UNDERCURRENTS

A Judgment Too Far? Judicial Activism
and the Constitution

UNDERCURRENTS

Other titles in the series

UNDERCURRENTS   Series Editor Carol Coulter

A Judgment Too Far? Judicial Activism and the Constitution

DAVID GWYNN MORGAN

CORK UNIVERSITY PRESS

First published in 2001 by
Cork University Press
University College
Cork
Ireland

British Library Cataloguing in Publication Data
A CIP catalogue record for this book is available from
the British Library

Library of Congress Cataloguing-in-Publication Data
Morgan, David Gwynn.
  A judgement too far? : judicial activism and the constitution / David Gwynn Morgan.
    p. cm. -- (Undercurrents ; no. 19)
  Includes bibliographical references and index.
  ISBN 1-85918-229-1 (pbk. : alk. paper)
   1. Judicial review--Ireland. 2. Political questions and judicial power--Ireland. I. Title.
  II. Undercurrents (Cork, Ireland); 19.

  KDK1713.M67 2001
  347.415'01c--dc21
                                                          2001047464
  ISBN 1 85918 229 1

Typeset by Tower Books, Ballincollig, Co. Cork
Printed by ColourBooks, Baldoyle, Co. Dublin

To Declan, Marie and Michael Cummins
and
Elystan and Alwen Morgan

Contents

Preface

The subject of this book – an audit of constitutional case-law and an attempt to see it in its political context – is far-flung and could, no doubt, have occupied a much larger number of pages. However, it is also a novel one – surprisingly so when one considers that the systematic treatment of pure constitutional law has now reached quite a venerable age: one thinks of J. Kelly, *Fundamental Rights in the Irish Law and Constitution* (1960), or even *The Constitution of the Irish Free State* (1932). And the *Undercurrents* series, with its brief span, is just the place to try out ideas, to throw up a target. Given the novelty of the subject matter, it seems good to try out the present set of ideas and opinions in a brief, tentative way, desite any loss in terms of intricacy or comprehensiveness that this may entail. Moreover, with length, the medium can often obscure the message. It is worth drawing these matters to the attention of the reader: 'Tread carefully for you tread on my reams.'

I should like to thank two colleagues and friends (whom I think it better not to name) who gave of their expertise and frankness to improve this book. I should also like to thank Ms Mary O'Regan and Ms Caroline Barrett, the secretaries who bore the brunt of word-processing several drafts of this book. Recall Pascal's remark: 'This letter is longer than usual because I have not had the time to make it shorter.'

May I also thank the staff of Cork University Press for their skill, dispatch and good humour. This is the fifth book in the *Undercurrents* series to have been written by a member of the UCC Law Department. This figure speaks well of each side, I think.

David Gwynn Morgan
St Swithin's Day, 2001

ix

Introduction

The role of the highest court in the field of government decisions and public policy making has been summarized as follows:

> The Supreme Court is thickly immersed in the formulation, implementation, and evaluation of public policy. Whether or not the authors of the Constitution intended it, many of the Court's judgments have political consequences. The Court's role differs from those of the other branches because its members are politically appointed, not elected. They are, however, bound to maintain the legitimacy of the institution of which they are members. Accordingly, its appointive character does not diminish the extent to which the Court is political, but modulates its expression.[1]

Curiously, while this summation is taken from a work on U.S. politics, it is broadly applicable here. Straightaway it raises this question: how is it that bodies, set up to settle cut and dried questions such as whether an accused is guilty of murder, or whether a defendant has established a right of way by long use, have come to decide major issues in such fields as taxation and foreign relations, education and health, trade licensing and compulsory acquisition?

Oddly enough the coming of judicial activism in the field of constitutional law-making has attracted relatively little discussion on the political plane. Comment in this area has consisted mainly of studies by lawyers (focusing on legal technique rather than the broader political and societal impact of judicial decisions); fulsome and ill-informed praise from the news media; and a gloomy silence from politicians, broken by only the occasional unreasoned squawk.

Yet it seems to me that this radical change raises a number of questions. First, in deciding on issues of constitutional interpretation, what values and sources of guidance do, or should, judges draw upon? More simply, what sections of the community win and what sections lose, by virtue of the judges'

1

decisions? Is there consistency from one judge to another? What is the quality of judicial craftsmanship in this new field? Given that this is an inherently political area, what rules have the judges devised to respect the pre-eminence of the executive and legislative branches?

These questions lead on to even broader issues. In view of the difference between the decision to be made in constitutional cases and in the traditional non-constitutional area, has there been any change in the framework of procedure within which the Court must operate? Again, do the broader waters into which the judges have swum call for a change in the system of selection of judges? Finally, since the membership of the higher courts is significant, recall that, during the period of just over a year commencing in September 1999, five new members were appointed to the eight-person Supreme Court and Keane J. became Chief Justice.[2] In what follows, I shall be using the term 'Keane Supreme Court' to describe the Court with its new membership. What difference has the new membership made?

All these queries involve subjects which come wearing a legal garb. But since judicial activism really involves the making of basic choices that affect the well-being of the community, it seems worthwhile to free them from their technical legal carapace and to comment on them in lay language. In addition, our approach here is not exclusively or mainly to decide what is the correct law, but rather what is good for the polity or community.

1. Judicial Activism

I Points of View

In the mid 1990s, I came across a friend - an intelligent lay person - who said: 'These days, I wonder whether our judges appreciate fully the impact of their actions, or do they think of the law as a thing apart which does not connect up with the real world?'

One of the examples my friend had in mind was the line of authority[1] which casts a doubt over the constitutionality of certain functions of District Court clerks, the administrators who play a crucial role in the running of the courts. This doubt flows from a line of cases centring upon Article 34.1 of the Constitution by which the judicial function may only be exercised by a judge. Now the argument which has found favour here is that when a court clerk is issuing a summons to appear before a court, he is exercising the judicial function and, since he is not a judge, this arrangement may be unconstitutional. Given that most of our criminal cases proceed through the District Court, the ramifications of this line of authority are immense.

Yet these cases overlook two points. First, a District Court clerk is under the Court's control and so might be regarded (as is the case in the corresponding situation in U.S. law) as an emanation of the judge, for the purpose of Article 34.1. Secondly, in defining the judicial function in regard to this provision, judges have held in other contexts, that one of the criteria for this difficult technical term is that the decision made should be final as to its consequences. Yet a summons merely calls a party before the Court: it does not decide on whether he is guilty or, if so, what his sentence should be. These are decisions for the judge himself to take later. In short, whether one examines the question from the perspective of legal technicality or from the wise policy that anything to do with a criminal conviction should be in the hands of an independent judge, this line of authority appears to have created doubts and difficulties which are unnecessary.

A second example of the same phenomenon to which my friend referred is the High Court decision in *Devanney v Minister for Justice* [1998] 1 LRM 593. The case centred this time upon the appointment of District Court clerks. According to the relevant legislation, these clerks are selected by the (politically neutral) Civil Service Commissioners but formally appointed by the Minister for Justice. The case focused on whether it was necessary, in order for this formal appointment to be valid, for it to be made personally by the Minister rather than (as had happened in this case) by a civil servant in the Department of Justice.

What is broadly speaking the same situation – the fact that the Minister was too busy and perhaps not an expert in the diverse areas covered by his department – had arisen elsewhere and an English judge had taken a common-sensical view: 'The collective knowledge, technical as well as factual, of the civil servants in the department and their collective experiences are to be treated as the Minister's own knowledge' (*Bushell v Secretary of State for the Environment* [1981] AC 75, 95).

In *Devanney*, however, the High Court took the opposite view – that the Minister ought to have made the appointments personally. In doing so, moreover, it ignored the Irish Supreme Court precedent of *Tang v Min. for Justice* [1996] ILRM 81, which concerned deportation, (not merely a formal act, as in *Devanney*). The consequences were far-reaching, since the validity of thousands of other summonses was also affected. Moreover, since summonses must be issued within six months of the offence, it would have been too late in most cases to issue fresh summonses.

In fact, the High Court decision in *Devanney* was reversed in the Supreme Court (a pattern we shall see repeated, fortunately) within a few weeks; but not before considerable public disquiet and loss of confidence had been engendered. And it was strange that matters had to go so far. For – and here is the important point – the High Court decision was not an instance of that phenomenon known as 'hard cases making bad law'. Rather, the point is that the law, dug up and enforced by the High Court, went back to the nineteenth century, when departments were small enough for Ministers to keep a finger in every pie. It had been disowned in the land of its birth; and had also been rejected in a number of pre-*Devanney* Irish cases. Its adoption by the High Court in *Devanney* was symptomatic of an apparently anti-executive attitude discernible in certain judicial decisions.

On the other hand, the judiciary has made many useful interventions, several of which are mentioned throughout the book and summarized in Chapter 10. Here we need mention only three examples. First, *McKenna v An Taoiseach (No. 2)* [1995] 2 IR 10, in which the Supreme Court held that a referendum to amend the Constitution is not fair if the Government spends public funds (about £500,000) on one side only of the campaign. *McKenna (No.2)* was followed in *Coughlan v Broadcasting Complaints Commission,* Supreme Court, 2 October 1999 which held that, at a referendum, RTE must allocate equal periods of uncontested broadcasting time to each side of the argument. (Anyone who supports a fair referendum process would have to see these cases as bringing an improvement).

Again, in *Brennan v Minister for Justice* [1995] 1 IR 612, the High Court struck down a totally unjustifiable, though long established, practice by which politicians had been interfering with the proper administration of justice by the courts. The facts were rather extreme: in 1993 (to take a typical year), 4,000 petitions had been made to the Minister for Justice for the remission or commutation of punishments (mainly fines) imposed in the criminal courts and some change had been made in well over half of these cases. Powers of this type are long established in Irish and British constitutional history, but only as an exceptional safety-valve against a failure of justice, by virtue of a too strict law or court procedure. Accordingly, they were retained in independent Ireland on the basis of the Constitution (Article 13.6) and the Criminal Justice Act 1951, s.6. But the High Court held, sensibly, that these powers are only to be used in exceptional cases, where (say) fresh evidence is discovered after the trial or where the quality of mercy should be allowed to prevail over the law. As Geoghegan J. remarked, with justifiable passion, the power of remission is not to be used to set up 'an alternative system of justice' (at p.628-29). (It is striking that the District Court often commits a sin similar to that of the Minister for Justice. This occurs when a judge makes it a condition of the application of the Probation of Offenders Act 1907 that the accused make a donation to the poor box, despite the fact that there is no such requirement in the Act. However no one seems to have taken a case to bar this practice. A week after *McKenna* (No. 2), the yes-side (that is, the Government side) won the Referendum by only 9,000 in a total vote of 1.5 million. Yet, curiously, the Supreme Court in *Hanafin v Miniser for the Environment* [1996] 2 I.L.R.M. 161, declined to upset the Referendum result.)

II Judicial Activism

It is appropriate at an early stage to say a little about 'judicial activism', a basic concept which is used rather freely, not least in this book. Now, as is well known, the higher judiciary (High or Supreme Court judges) has two types of function. The first is to determine the facts of the case and to apply the existing law (common law or act of the Oireachtas) to them, in order to decide the case before them. This function can certainly sometimes involve the application of existing law in ways which are unexpected or are unwelcome to the Government or some interest group. Thus, for example, the army deafness claims involve a huge bill for damages against the State but do not result from any new rule of law, merely an application of existing law to novel facts. On the plane of principle, this line of cases is an example of the independence of the judiciary; but not of judicial activism. And so we shall not pursue cases of this sort any further.

This book is mainly concerned with the second function. This consists of the striking down of a law or action when the judges find it to be inconsistent with the Constitution. Here, there are two possibilities: first, in some cases – given the content of the law under review and the Constitution – striking down a law will simply be a technical operation, requiring the competent and honest application of generally accepted rules. Some examples of this sort of case are given later in the present chapter. Making Ireland fertile ground for cases of this type is the fact that many of our laws and institutions were instituted pre-Independence, and until the 1990s remarkably little had been done (in comparison with Britain and other foreign jurisdictions) in the public law field by the political organs by way of reform. The judiciary was thus left as, in effect, the main body willing and able to perform this task and, in doing so, it could go some substantial distance on a non-controversial diet of modernization without having to negotiate difficult policy choices. One example: in his radical programme of law reform, announced in 1966, the Minister for Justice Mr Haughey, announced with a fanfare of trumpets that he intended to uproot the ancient rule of the Royal Prerogative, by which (statutory exceptions apart) the State was immune from any action in tort. Yet, as far as the political organs were concerned, the rest was silence. It was left to the Supreme Court (in *Byrne v Ireland* [1972] IR 241) to remove this archaic law. On the other hand, legal technique only takes one so far. As has been remarked: 'The fundamental error of recent political philosophy is to imagine that conflicts of value can be marginalized by adopting an agreed idea of justice'.[2] Thus there is a second category of case, in which – in order to resolve the case one way or the other – a judge has to call on some element of policy choice or preference. In this sort of case, if the judge selects the option of not accepting the status quo as it is given in the form of law or government action, but instead strikes down the law or action as unconstitutional, then the judge is (on the definition in use here) performing an act of 'judicial activism'.

The great question is this: in cases of judicial activism, what source or sources of guidance do judges draw upon? Various sources, appealing to different judges, have been suggested. An early view is that the Constitution should be interpreted in the light of natural law values, and even that any constitutional provision or amendment that is in conflict with natural law is invalid. However, this view was decisively rejected in *Re Art. 26 and the Regulation of Abortion Information Bill 1995* [1995] I.I.R.I.[3] A second line of thought which has been identifed as underpinning judical decisons is 'liberal democracy,' a philosphy that sets a heavy value on the freedom of choice of the individual and his right to be 'let alone' by the State, in such areas as privacy and property. A third set of tenets has been called 'communitaranism'. This prizes those shared ends which define the community's way of life. These include the proper functioning of the legal and democractic political systems; the protection of minority or disadvantaged groups; and even the positive application of economic and social rights. Cutting across these three approaches, there are, as we shall learn, different views as to how activist it is appropriate for judges to be.[4]

I shall return to this question in Chapter 10 (at pp. 106–9). But what can be said now is that the notion that there is no need for judicial policy-making since the policy is to be found in the Constitution and the invalidating of a law merely flows automatically from an 'interpretation' of the Constitution, is often unrealistic, for the reason that clear-cut guidance from the Constitution is often simply not available. Moreover such an approach would beg several questions, notably what rule of interpretation has been selected by the judge? (On which issue see Chapter 9). For the moment therefore, let us agree that in some constitutional cases, an act of selection by the judge beyond the mere deployment of the skills of legal technique is called for, and if s/he makes the positive choice of departing from the path adopted by the legislative or executive, we may call this judicial activism.[5] Furthermore, to return to a difficulty that was glided over earlier, even the application of legal techniques, especially in an area like constitutional law, in which doctrine is not well-established, is by no means uncontroversial. Likewise, the boundary between the two categories of case just identified – those in which a straightforward reading of the Consitution coupled with legal technique points to a particular result and those in which it does not – is frequently that between varying shades of grey. In other words, it is itself a matter of controversy. In addition I shall also have some remarks to make about the operation of technical legal craft-skill in this newish field.

There is another dimension in which the judiciary have been increasingly activist. At first, judicial review was simply negative in the sense that laws or actions were struck down. By now, we have seen a number of cases, for example Sinnott, in which the Constitution was used to impose a positive duty on the State. One significant difference is that this positive usage requires a judge to determine what is appropriate in a particular context – education in Sinnott – and this calls for greater knowledge and creativity than simply striking down.

The undoubted extension of the judge's authority that judicial activism represents is sometimes justified by reference to the inadequacy of politicians and the political system. Whether politicians are inadequate is a difficult question, when one takes into account the strains imposed (more or less legitimately) on them in a mass democracy. Recall Churchill's observation that 'Democracy is the worst form of government; except all those other forms of government that have been tried from time to time.' Bear in mind, too, the rough and ready notion that people get the politicians they deserve: they did, after all, vote for them. This is a question which is beyond the terms of reference of this book and the ken of this author. But it bears mentioning in order to emphasize the fact that there are good reasons why politicians are as they are and may be unable to meet the rather high standards set by judges, who inhabit a rather different and secluded world. This point is worth making, however glancingly, because a main project of the judiciary seems to flow from the major unspoken premise that it is only the courts which can be trusted to take certain of society's major decisions. I make this assumption because it is the best way to explain the substantial reservoir of power for which the higher judiciary has taken responsibility. In the remainder of this book, I shall illustrate this taking of responsibility at many points.

III The Constitution

This is not a book about the Constitution; but about the use to which the judges have put it. However given the criticisms made of the Constitution in some quarters – out of date, illiberal, even sectarian, even illiberal – it is worthwhile stating that the raw material with which the judges work is, in many ways, a wise and far-sighted document. The survey on which the following assessment is based is a comparison between the Constitution and the European Convention on Human Rights, from which the former emerges surprisingly well. Following his survey, the writer concludes:

> As the Constitution is often – erroneously – supposed to have been the handiwork of just one man, Eamon de Valera, it is naturally assumed in many non-legal quarters that it entirely reflects the values of Hibernia Irredenta: the narrow, authortitarian, Gaelic Catholic ethos which prevailed at the time. While the Constitution still does in places reflect these values, the fact that it has survived and is thriving in a modern and very different era is testament to the fact that it transcended those cultural values of the 1930s.[6]

In short, the instrument is sound and we may concentrate on the performance.

IV Independence of the Judiciary

For the remainder of this chapter, I propose to deal with two discrete points: the independence of the judiciary and nation-building. It is a necessary condition for judicial activism (though not the only one) that judges should be independent of pressure from the Government or any other source. On the question of judicial independence, Dr Blathna Ruane concludes, after a thorough study of the period 1922–1987:

> Overall the documentation examined and information gathered from interviews suggests that despite these pressures on the independence of members of the Court the politicians have not attempted to interfere with their decision-making. The writer has not found any evidence from these sources, of impropriety in judicial decision-making and indeed the behind-the-scenes evidence

suggests that the judges, regardless of their former political affiliations, have been careful to protect their
independence and indeed take considerable pride and
derive a sense of prestige from their independent status.
Peer pressure and a sense of their own constitutional
role in power seemed to be important factors in but-
tressing judicial independence. This behind-the-scenes
evidence of judicial independence is also borne out by
an examination of how the Court has dealt with important and controversial constitutional cases.[7]

This view is confirmed by many of the cases outlined in the
present pamphlet and, it may be said, it is the view of almost
everyone who has studied the subject that the independence of
the Irish judiciary has never been in question. This was evident
long before the era of judicial activitism. Take, for instance, *The
State (Burke) v Lennon* [1940] IR136 in which Gavan Duffy J. held
sections of the Offences Against the State Act 1939, providing
for the internment of suspected subversives, unconstitutional.
This decision resulted in the release of certain persons who went
on, a week later, to make a successful raid on a government
ammunition dump. As another piece of evidence, take the
following, rather characteristic, remark of Mr Justice Walsh in a
newspaper interview to mark his retirement:

> Nevertheless you must give the decision, *ruat coelum*.
> For example there was an affidavit submitted [in the
> *Crotty* case] by the Department of Foreign Affairs which
> said that other Member States were very cross with us
> – totally irrelevant, certainly we're not concerned about
> what other people think, and if they think badly of us,
> they should think badly of the Dáil or of the
> Government . . .[8]

Sometimes, the judge's independence has been taken to an
extreme. Take, for instance, the judges' disapproval of the Article
26 reference procedure which is, after all, a basic part of the
Constitution. The Supreme Court gave vent to these feelings in a
judgment, nearly a third of which consists of an attack on the

Article 26 procedure and which amounted, according to one writer, to 'an implicit request to the President that no similar Bills should be sent to the court in future'.[9]

Despite such episodes, the executive has been generally respectful of the judiciary's independence. In 1936, for instance, Mr de Valera did not seize the opportunity that presented itself, by virtue of the enlargement of the Supreme Court from three to five members (in the Courts of Justice Act 1936) and the more or less simultaneous death of Kennedy C.J., to pack the Court.[10] Moreover, as is well known, Sean Lemass consciously initiated the era of judicial activism as part of his project of modernizing Ireland, by his selection of Ó Dálaigh C.J. and Walsh J. and by his private admonition to each of them, on appointment (on the same day in 1961), that he 'would like the Supreme Court to become more like the United States Supreme Court'. Recollecting both this interview and his own appointment, Mr Justice Walsh remarked that 'the horse was chosen for the course'.[11] Again, we have had, in Ireland, no equivalent of such infringements of judicial independence as the Italian constitutional amendment of 1987, removing the shield against legal action against judges for grave errors; the (British) Lord Chancellor's letter leading to the resignation of the President of the Employment Appeal Tribunal;[12] the Indian supercession of judges;[13] or even, in an analogous field in Ireland, the insult to President Ó Dálaigh which led to his resignation in October 1976.

There is no doubt that, in many areas, the judiciary's influence has been most constructive. It has, for instance, taken a strong and consistent line in regard to the 'Rule of Law', which I take to mean that everyone, especially the State and its organs, is subject to the law and the Constitution; that the law must be public and precise; and that the law and Constitution must be enforced by independent judges. Judicial intolerance of the executive acting above the law may be illustrated by *The State (Quinn) v Ryan* [1965] IR 70, which stemmed from the extradition arrangements established by the Petty Sessions (Ir) Act 1851, when Ireland was part of the United Kingdom. This heirloom meant that there was a system for extradition from Ireland to the U.K. which allowed no opportunity for the person sought to have the legality of his arrest and extradition tested by a court, before being (as in the *Quinn* case) whisked over the border. Condemning this system, Ó Dálaigh C.J. stated (at 105): '. . . no one can with impunity set these [fundamental] rights at nought and the Courts' powers in this regard are as ample as the defence of the Constitution requires'. Possibly the judges' strongest stance in the field of criminal procedure has been in regard to the Special Criminal Court. As enacted, the legislation establishing this Court provided for substantial curtailment of the rights usually enjoyed by the accused. However, as operated by the judges, trial before the Court has not been all that different from that before a conventional court.[14] Next (long before the matter was settled by amendment of the Constitution), the judges had established a steady line of authority that it was for the court, and not the Minister, to decide when the interest in the confidentiality of executive documents (or other information) justified the exclusion of evidence which would be relevant in court proceedings.[15] Most recently, the courts have intervened significantly to strike down deportation on the broad grounds that non-natural parents cannot be deported if they have an Irish-born child, a more liberal law than is to be found in any other State *(Fajujonu v Min. for Justice* [1990] ILRM 234). Again the Minister for Justice had been granted, by the Aliens Act 1935, an unguided discretion in this sensitive area *(Laurentiu v Minister for Justice* [2000] 1 ILRM 1) and again, this was struck down by the Supreme Court. In addition, the High Court has struck down the Director of Public Prosecutions's decision to change his mind and bring a prosecution for dangerous driving, following receipt of a letter from the victim of the family of the deceased.[16]

V Nation Building

One of the positive ways in which the judges have influenced the law and legal system is by helping to 'nationalize' or 'indigenize' it, thereby contributing to the State's self-confidence and integrity.[17] This is a more significant achievement than it might at first appear. In 1922, the newly-independent Irish Free State naturally commenced life with the laws of the former colonial power; the alternative would have been anarchy since the Brehon laws had been effectively cut off by the late sixteenth-century *Tanistry* case and anyway would have been unsuitable for twentieth-century society. For the first forty or more years, very little happened to distinguish the post-Independence system of laws from its predecessor. There is nothing strange about this inactivity. Ireland was a small island next to, and very much under the cultural influence of, what was at first a major, then later a medium, world power, which was also acknowledged as the mother of the common law, which had spawned children in all parts of the globe. Ireland's legal profession and judicial system were modelled on the tried and tested British model and it had next to no legal text books of its own. It was natural, therefore, that legislation should be modelled on the British counterpart and that until the recent decades, British precedents should be regarded as binding. Moreover, especially during the past twenty or thirty years, the grain of history had seemed to be working against any need for a differentiation in the laws. Various socio-economic developments in Ireland worked to bring the two societies closer together. So, too, did the intensification of EU membership.

Yet against this background the Irish judiciary, in the 1960s and the 1970s, launched two distinctive initiatives, the first being the introduction of a strong form of judicial review of laws and governmental actions and the other being the huge improvement in the prospects of the plaintiff in an action for personal injuries. In several other ways, too, the judiciary shaped a distinctive legal system which was suitable to Irish needs and values. In *AG v Ryan's Car Hire* [1965] IR 642, Walsh J. rejected the argument that 'because the Courts had taken over the English common law, accordingly they must adopt the English approach to constitutional cases' and stated that U.S. authorities were a more suitable guide. In addition, Ireland's experience as a de facto colony had created an instinctive sympathy for the underdog reflected by the legal system in a greater sympathy for the weaker party in relations between landlord and tenant; employer and employee; insurer and insured. Likewise, the Irish criminal justice system has always been even more slanted in favour of the accused than that of Britain. In summary, the Irish judges helped to establish a legal system which the ordinary Irish citizen could feel that s/he – to use the vivid, contemporary metaphor – 'owned' rather than regarding it as something which had been designed by foreign specialists. Given the drift towards alienation from institutions of government and the practical importance of a feeling of a moral obligation to obey law, this achievement must be regarded as a significant piece of nation-building.

2. The Common Law Judge

I Development of the judge as law-maker

Before coming to the main part of this book – the interpretation and application of the Constitution – we need to consider briefly the assumptions about the role of the judges in making the common law and interpreting statute. For it is this original role – widely and correctly respected – which has shaped the view taken by judges (and others) of the courts' task in the constitutional field, despite the fact that this is such a different sphere.

To explain the role of the higher judiciary as law-makers, we need to take on board a modicum of history. To over-simplify, until the nineteenth century (with the coming of 'big government' and the welfare state), the Government's duties were stringently confined to maintaining law and order and carrying on foreign relations. Thus, for good or for ill, the Government made much less impact on the affairs of its citizens and accordingly there was little need for public law, that is the law that regulates the

State and its relations with citizens. Take next private law, or the law controlling relations between private citizens – for instance, contract, tort, and property: in an era when society changed very slowly few people litigated and there was less concern for 'injustice' than there is today. The result was that there was little call for legislative change.

Accordingly, the significant point for present purposes is that, until the mid nineteenth century, such change in the law as did occur was gradual and incremental and came about largely through case-law, which was in the hands of the higher judiciary. And this remains the case for large tracts of law.

For many centuries, the consensus of the time was that judges did not make, but merely 'declared', law, i.e. made manifest in the context of some concrete case a rule which had really existed all the time. Lord Devlin guyed this fiction in the following classic passage:

> There was a time when it was thought almost indecent to suggest that judges make law – they only declared it. Those with a taste for fairy tales seem to have thought that in some Aladdin's cave there is hidden the Common Law in all its splendour and that on a judge's appointment there depends on him knowledge of the magic words 'Open Sesame'. . . . But we do not believe in fairy tales any more.[1]

This fictional view of what was happening persisted for a surprisingly long period because it suited the interests of many parties. It suited the judges because it helped to uphold their image as being detached from, and somehow 'above', politics (a point to which we must return). And it suited politicians – whether Ministers or legislators – because it fortified the message that theirs were the critical decisions in shaping the legal system. It was also reassuring to the susceptibilities of litigants involved in particular cases, who might have been shocked to discover that the public function of law-making was in fact being carried out at their expense.

Certain points emerge from this lightning historical sketch that are of relevance to the Irish polity even at the turn of the millennium. It is true that the traditional tenet was that judges do not 'make' law. This is, by now, a rather old-fashioned belief with (I should guess) a minority of adherents among informed people. Nevertheless, it is connected with the correct view that what judges do is a less radical form of law-making than that of the legislature. Important consequences flow from this. First, it is accepted that, in the exercise of their limited law-making functions, judges do not need to be expert in the field affected by the law-making, be it economic, scientific, sociological, architectural, etc. Nor need they call evidence in these fields from experts. Secondly, the focus is almost exclusively on the parties who happen to have come before the court: their behaviour, their circumstances and the consequences of the decision for them. None of the wider ramifications of the decision are before the court. Nor, thirdly, is machinery available by which the judges can receive representations from groups affected by their law-making, as occurs when law is changed by legislation, as a result either of lobbying of the relevant ministers and departments by interest groups, or of speeches in the Houses of the Oireachtas by elected members speaking on behalf of constituents or others affected. A comparison of judicial and legislative law-making in the same field is afforded by the changes in the law relating to negligence of landowners and their responsibility to persons trespassing on the land. These changes came about through three court cases taken by youngsters who had been hurt while trespassing on land owned by the defendants. This had the effect of shifting the law in favour of the trespasser and against the landowners. Legislation was called for. When it came to legislation reforming this area, the process was more thorough and representative than in the earlier bout of judicial law-making. Initially, there was a reference of the issue for review by the Law Reform Commission. Eventually, following a period of reflection by the Government, after considering submissions from interest groups, a Bill was published. And, after debate in the Oireachtas, it was enacted.[2]

A final point concerns Article 15.2.1° (an aspect of the Separation of Powers, which bans law-making by any body other than the Oireachtas). This provision has been taken seriously by the judges in constitutional cases involving laws made in the form of regulations, by ministers, under authority delegated to them by act of the Oireachtas. Yet when it comes to judicial law-making by the common law (as contrasted with the interpretation of legislation), very little interest has been shown in the question of how this form of law can continue to exist in the light of Article 15.2.1°. But if one does confront the question squarely, the only possible answer is that if common law law-making can be reconciled with the Constitution, this can be done solely on the basis that it is confined to whatever incremental extension of the law is necessary to resolve the concrete facts before the court. Yet the change in the law on trespassers – to take an example mentioned just now – seems to have been a substantial change of principle. Was it not, therefore, unconstitutional?

To summarize: judicial law-making suffers from various flaws; the judges are not necessarily experts in the subject area affected by the law, and they approach the issue from the perspective of the (possibly unrepresentative) parties before the court.

II Doctrine of precedent

In respect of each of these features of judicial law-making (whether constitutional or not), the conventional response has been to say that they are unimportant for the reason that such law-making is incremental only. Like much conventional wisdom, this is no doubt correct. But, if judicial law-making is to be only 'incremental', the achievement of this result depends – apart from judicial self-restraint – upon the fundamental watchword in this area, which is the doctrine of precedent. This doctrine is an inherently simple notion which, indeed, is followed not just by the courts but by almost all large institutions (for example: insurance companies dealing with policy holders; local authorities dealing with corporation tenants; universities dealing with students). What the doctrine means is that once a ruling has been made in respect of a particular situation, it should be applied in all later examples of the same situation.

But, as the alert reader will speedily point out, there is more to it than that. Apart from genuinely 'open' points, the precedent system leaves elbow-room for flexibility or judicial creativity on a number of fronts. Since extracting the true rule of law from a previous authority involves an exercise in generalization, a margin of appreciation is left to the judge. For instance, the judge in the later case may focus on the particular circumstances of the two cases and perceive some feature which requires him to 'distinguish' the earlier case from the one before him. Again, the precedent may date from an age when the needs and values underpinning the law – be they scientific, moral or commercial – were so different as to render the precedent less compelling.

But the existence of this sort of exception does not mean that the doctrine of precedent should cease to be the general principle that is followed in most cases. Precedent is one of the central elements in judge-craft because it gives certainty and hence predictability, which is the quality that enables lawyers on opposing sides to give their respective clients the same view of the law, so that every dispute does not have to end up in court. Again, justice is difficult to achieve because of its subjectivity and because of the all-encompassing field of history and circumstances which the search for justice opens up. But certainty is attainable and the doctrine of precedent is the basic tool by which it has been secured. Following the doctrine, a judge sacrifices his own view of what is just or desirable and instead, honours his judicial oath of office to 'uphold the constitution and the laws' (Article 34.5). If precedent is not followed, the observer is likely to think that the judge has been moved by some personal policy, preference or belief. This is particularly significant in the constitutional field for reasons explained at pp. 109-10.

Unfortunately judicial practice over the past two decades shows numerous cases of judges ignoring this basic precept. This is true of all areas, but especially in the constitutional field. Two examples are given elsewhere.[3] Here let us summarize another two.

The first pair of cases is *The People (D.P.P.) v O'Shea* [1982] IR 384 and *The People (DPP) v Quilligan (No 2)* [1989] ILRM 245. *O'Shea* interpreted Article 34.43 literally to hold that an appeal does lie to the Supreme Court from an acquittal in the High Court. In *Quilligan*, the immediate question was whether the jurisdiction to hear an appeal against acquittal carries with it the power to order a fresh trial. If one accepts *O'Shea*, it seems impossible to deny that this is so; yet in *Quilligan*, the Supreme Court did so. It is plain from the judgments in *Quilligan* that the case really amounted to a reversal of *O'Shea*, which had been decided only a few years before. No change in circumstances was adduced to justify this shift.

The second example concerns international affairs: in the significant case of *Crotty v An Taoiseach* [1987] IR 713, Crotty, the plaintiff, sought an order restraining the Government from ratifying the Single European Act, the critical parts of which provided for improved co-operation among EU Member States in the sphere of foreign policy. The plaintiff's successful argument was that since Article 29.4 vests the Government with the power to conduct foreign affairs, it is not open to the State to fetter the Government's authority by a Treaty (the SEA), which would oblige it to make foreign policy with a greater measure of co-operation with other nations of the EEC. The contrasting case, *McGimpsey v Ireland* [1990] 1 IR 11, was equally politically charged. Here the plaintiff sought a declaration that the Anglo-Irish Agreement of 1985 was unconstitutional. The Agreement constituted the Anglo-Irish Inter-Governmental Conference through which the British and Irish Governments could seek to align their policies in relation to Northern Ireland. This, the plaintiff submitted, was unconstitutional because, as in *Crotty*, there was a violation of the provision vesting authority in foreign affairs exclusively in the Irish Government.

Confirmation of this weakening observance of precedent and (given the fact that this weakening extends outside the constitutional area) a slightly generous explanation for it is contained in the following remarks of John D. Cooke (at the time of the remarks, a Senior Counsel and now a member of the Court of First Instance of the European Communities):

> I have a sneaking suspicion that one of the effects of the Constitution upon the way in which the law is practised in this country has been to introduce an element of indiscipline, looseness and even laziness. For one thing, the Constitution was entirely our own creation and its effects in particular judgments or decisions were not subject to any outside appeal or scrutiny or to comparison with parallel developments elsewhere. Moreover, the code of constitutional law lends itself to general propositions and the making of decisions by reference to broadly-drawn principles . . . Most practitioners would, I suspect, acknowledge that the different approach which has been conditioned by the constitutional background in this country produces greater fairness and renders judgments frequently more realistic and compassionate by giving the judiciary an opportunity to be less confined by strict and literal rules of interpretation and of the strait-jacket of precedent.
>
> Nevertheless, I think it has also contributed to a loss of the discipline of reasoning that would formerly have been so typical of the common law approach to the arguing of legal issues by reference to precedent. It is relatively rare nowadays in the Irish courts that you see the fully-fledged performance of the intellectual exercise involved in arguing a point by reference to precedent. The disciplined exercise of tracing the development of a particular point by analysing carefully the legal rationale through a long series of cases is not always well received in the modern Irish court. Your typical High Court action will frequently dispose of the legal argument by a reference to one or two older reported cases supplemented by a jump to one or two recent and, preferably, unreported judgments.[4]

Another shaft of criticism which obliquely encompasses the way the Constitution has been employed and the decline in the use of precedents comes from the field of criminal law. Professor McAuley and Dr McCutcheon write:

> In Ireland [there has been a] virtual eclipse of substantive criminal appeals by the blinding star - of constitutional justice. Although this development is to some extent a natural consequence of the overriding importance of fundamental rights and fair procedures under the Constitution, it has had a disastrous effect on Irish criminal law, stunting its natural development and leaving those charged with its administration to fend as best they can on a diet of first-instance rulings and directions, as supplemented by English authority . . . Criminal law states seem destined to remain bereft of an accompanying jurisprudence explaining their key terms and elucidating their linkages with the general principles of criminal liability as understood and applied by the Irish courts. There is also the national scandal that the decisions of the Court of Criminal Appeal, such as they are, are not systematically reported, not to mention the dismal refrain, ubiquitous in legal circles – and sometimes heard, albeit sotto voce, even from judicial lips – that this odd arrangement has the dark merit of stilling the ridicule that the ratiocinations of that court might otherwise provoke from incredulous observers.[5]

The rest of this book is confined to constitutional law. These lengthy quotations are included to show that the sort of comments made here are not particular to constitutional law, though they may apply most strongly to it.

3. Sexual and Social Mores

The judges' reputation as a liberalizing and modernizing force rests to a large extent on their work in the field covered in the present chapter. However, as we shall see from this brief survey of some decisions in the field of contraception, abortion, homo-sexuality and adoption, this reputation depends primarily on the first area only. Elsewhere, the record is rather patchy.

I Contraception

Mrs McGee had a medical condition which meant that any further pregnancy might be fatal. Her doctor recommended a contraceptive. However, the time was the 1970s and the Criminal Law Amendment Act 1935 made the sale or import of contraceptives a criminal offence. Accordingly, a packet containing Mrs McGee's contraceptives was seized by the customs authorities. Mrs McGee then successfully challenged the constitutionality of the ban contained in the 1935 Act in the Supreme Court (*McGee v A.G.* [1974] IR 284).

Although the point is not entirely clear, it seems that it was Mrs McGee's status as a married woman, rather than her medical condition, which was essential to her success. According to Walsh J. (at p. 312):

> The sexual life of a husband and wife is of necessity and by its nature an area of particular privacy. If the husband and wife decide to limit their family or to avoid having children by use of contraceptives, it is a matter peculiarly within the joint decision of the husband and wife and one into which the State cannot intrude, unless its intrusion can be justified by the exigencies of the common good. The question of whether the use of contraceptives by married couples within their marriage is or is not contrary to the moral code to which they subscribe . . . could not justify State intervention. Similarly, the fact that the use of contraceptives may offend against the moral code of the majority of the citizens of the State would not *per se* justify an intervention by the State to prohibit their use within marriage.

In the present context, two comments, one positive and the other negative, may be made about the performance of the judges in *McGee*. As to the first point, it is only necessary to mention the political background to *McGee* in order to emphasize the courageous and radical character of the decision. As soon as contraceptives began to be in any way widely available, they had been banned by the Criminal Law Amendment Act 1935. Even in the late 60s and 70s, the only political attempt at reform was three (defeated) Private Members Bills. (The 1969 measure proposed by Senator Mary Robinson was so unpopular that the Senate took the most unusual step of denying permission to have it printed and circulated). Furthermore, when, in 1974, the Government introduced a measure to reform the law in the light of the *McGee* decision, the measure failed, with the Taoiseach and the Minister of Education actually joining the opposition to it. Thus it might well be said that, in taking this decisive action, the Courts were courageously fulfilling one of their duties, namely to use open-textured areas of the Constitution to keep the laws up to date and in line with the changing needs and values of society, in a situation in which the principal guarantor – the legislature – appeared reluctant to act. The judges were thereby upholding a significant and legitimate personal right.

II Abortion

As regards the second comment, there was a price to be paid for *McGee*. This was the impact which the decision made in the field of abortion, an impact which flowed directly from the quality of judicial activism with which *McGee* was loaded. To put it simply, opponents of abortion considered it at least possible that the Court, having discerned a right to contraception in an open area of the Constitution, might find a right to abortion in the same source. Despite the fact that members of the Court went out of their way to say that this path would not be taken, this feeling inspired political pressure which led eventually to the Eighth Amendment of the Constitution (the so-called pro-life Amendment) of 1983 which implanted Article 40.3.3° in the

Constitution. Given the character of the reasoning in *McGee*, it is hard to say that this fear was altogether unreasonable, bearing in mind that the sequence of events the Amendment was intended to guard against had in fact been followed by the U.S. Supreme Court in the well-known cases of *Griswold v Connecticut* 381 U.S. 79 (1965) (contraception) leading on to *Roe v Wade* 410 U.S. 113 (1973) (abortion).

It is convenient now to turn to the Court's record in the field of abortion and the Eighth Amendment. The Amendment provides: 'The State acknowledges the right to life of the unborn and, *with due regard to the equal right to life of the mother*, guarantees in its laws to respect, and, as far as practicable, by its laws to defend and vindicate that right' (my emphasis).

The first series of cases which drew upon Article 40.3.3° consisted of attempts by the supporter of the Amendment to prevent the operation, in Ireland, of abortion referral services advising pregnant women about abortion facilities in Britain. We shall pursue this topic no further here other than to note that, given the fairly stringent wording of the provisions, it is hard to see what the judges could or should have done other than to grant the orders sought, which is – on the whole – what they did.

The main case here, however, is *Attorney General v X* [1992] I.R.1. Such was the interest in the case that the judgments plus arguments were published in a separate volume.[1] Here the Attorney General sought – unsuccessfully before the Supreme Court – an injunction to restrain a 14-year-old girl, pregnant as a result of what was then believed to be a rape by a middle-aged man, from travelling to Britain for an abortion. The central point of the case was the danger that the mother would commit suicide if she were obliged to carry the baby to term. This enabled a four to one majority of the Supreme Court to find that the element of the Eighth Amendment which speaks of 'the equal right to life of the mother' was engaged and, thus, to hold that an injunction to restrain the defendant mother from travelling should not be granted.

In this very brief analysis, two points should be emphasized.

First of all, the Supreme Court majority radically reinterpreted the words just quoted – in particular the word, 'equal' – so as to mean that there had to be 'real and substantial' risk to the life of the mother. It seems to be reasonable to depart from a literal reading here since – to employ the generally accepted test as to when such a departure is permissible – a literal reading would lead to an absurdity.

But it is less easy to justify that Court's reasoning on the second point, which is whether – on the facts of the case – this test was actually satisfied by the threat of suicide. As Kelly remarks: 'What is surprising about the majority judgments, however, is the manner in which they equate the threat of suicide with life-threatening conditions of a physical nature as a real and substantial risk. Regrettably none of the majority judgments go into any detail in defending this equation'.[2] To put the same point from a slightly different perspective: elsewhere in the law some such doctrine as 'waiver' is imported so that the owner of a legal right cannot turn around and claim to rely on a right which he (or she) has attempted to undermine. Yet, in this case, X was allowed to invoke the right to life while herself threatening suicide. A further difference between a life-threatening illness and a threat of suicide lies in the practical possibility of averting the former by taking appropriate measures (this being the basis of Hederman J.'s dissent in the case.)

In response to this line of argument, it might be objected that in reality (as opposed to the wording of their judgments) the Supreme Court majority may have been moved by a humanitarian concern for the plight of the 14-year-old girl; and, also, that it could be said that when the people passed the Amendment in 1983, they certainly did not envisage it as concerning such extreme circumstances as arose in the *X* case. Moreover, one should also mention the extraordinary torrent of feeling (mainly in favour of letting 'the young girl go to Britain') on the issue, which erupted at all levels of society (bus-stops, pubs, etc.) during the three-week period between the High and Supreme Court judgments.[3] It would be perverse to think that the judges were unaware or unaffected.

Yet, as against this, it must be said that public sentiment is an elusive and subjective consideration and a court should not rest its decision upon such a basis. If it does so, at the very least it should be alert to the possibility of creating a classic instance of the danger identified by the adage 'hard cases make bad law'. In short, given that the Court intended to reach the decision which it did, it should have done so on a narrow basis confined to the extreme circumstances of the *X* case rather than hauling out into the broad waters represented by the idea of an exception based on a threat of suicide, which seems to grant a wide latitude for the subversion of a constitutional provision voted by a recent and large majority of the people. For instance, it should have been possible to avoid this result by grounding the decision on the technical law relating to wards of court (since X was a minor) or injunctions (since an injunction to restrain her from leaving the jurisdiction was involved). Seen in this light, there seems to have been a lack of thought behind the majority judgments. Or as Kelly remarks: '[The decision's] foundations . . . could have been dug more deeply'.

There is a further point. One traditional way of dealing with the dilemma at the heart of the *X* case would have been for the Attorney General to exercise his discretion not to seek the injunction in the first place. Such a discretion exists just because the Attorney General is both a political and legal personage. Consequently he has always been regarded as having the wisdom and responsibility to exercise such a discretion in the rare cases in which, though the law might allow a legal action, humanitarian or other considerations are so overwhelming as to justify not taking legal action. Yet, in regard even to the young defendant in *X*, the Attorney General claimed that he had no discretion to abstain from action on the ground that a constitutional right was involved. And, in *X*, the Supreme Court remarked ([1992] IR at 46–47) *obiter* that this was the correct view. Given the kaleidoscope of circumstances which can engage a constitutional right – going, of course, way beyond abortion – this was a rash remark (unsubstantiated by principle or, since it was the first time the issue had been considered, precedent) from which the Court would have done well to abstain and which may land future Attorneys General and others in trouble.

III Homosexuality

In *Norris v A.G.* [1985] IR 36 a practising homosexual argued unsuccessfully that the nineteenth-century statutes that made male homosexual activity in private a criminal offence, were unconstitutional. His argument, which relied in part on *McGee* as a precedent, failed in the Supreme Court, by a majority of 3:2. It may seem tempting to criticize the majority on the basis that, since the results in *Norris* and *McGee* were different in respect of somewhat similar sexual/moral issues, consequently the Court (with a similar membership) was guilty of an inconsistency. In assessing this criticism, one should note first that no more in *McGee* than in *Norris* did the Court follow the precept that this was an issue best left to the legislature. Rather, in each case it addressed the issue directly and itself weighed the privacy right against community morality. However, it dealt rather differently with community morality in the two cases. In *McGee*, there was no real focus on this side of the scales. By contrast, in *Norris*, the majority of the Court went into the supposed effects of homosexuality on society in more detail (risk to public health; undermining marriage; suicide). But their treatment of the evidence was not very impressive. The central fact is that Mr Norris had called ten experts in, variously, psychiatry, sociology and theology to testify – in short – that homosexual practice was not socially damaging. By contrast, the Attorney General had called no evidence in response to defend the constitutionality of the nineteenth-century statutes.

In these circumstances, the legally correct course for the Court – in line with the accusatorial character of its procedure – would have been to accept Mr Norris's uncontradicted evidence. Instead, the majority of the court drew upon what seemed to be their own views. (This line of criticism will be found in the minority judgments (at pp. 76–77, 102)).

The real ground of the decision may have been that judges decided that Irish society was not, at that point, ready for a change; whereas it believed the opposite in *McGee*.

One further point concerns the majority's failure to pay heed to the European Convention on Human Rights. The background to this is that the law criminalizing homosexuality was the pre-Independence legislation, common to Britain (though repealed there in 1967) and both parts of Ireland. However, in 1981 in *Dudgeon v U.K.* 5 EHRR 573, the European Court of Human Rights had ruled, in the context of Northern Ireland, that this law violated the right to privacy protected by Article 8(1) of the Convention. In the light of *Dudgeon*, it was clear that the Irish Law could not withstand a challenge in the European Court (as was confirmed a few years later in *Norris v Ireland* (1989) 13 EHRR 186).

It might be asked then why the Supreme Court did not save everyone the delay and embarrassment of a trip to the European Court? The correct technical answer to this question – which was given by the majority – lies in the fact that the European Convention is not part of Irish law and hence, as a result of Article 29.6, cannot be taken account of in an Irish court. And yet there have been other cases[4] in which, when dealing with open questions on the interpretation of the Irish Constitution, the courts here have been prepared to take into account the interpretation of a comparable provision in the Convention. Given the closeness of the Given the closeness of the *Dudgeon* decision of the European Court, *Norris* might have seemed an especially appropriate situation for such recourse.

IV Adoption

Although the material circumstances of the country have changed radically since the first Adoption Act was passed in 1952, adoption remains a very sensitive area. Today, most of the adopted children are from impoverished, foreign jurisdictions many of them culturally very different from Ireland. But the circumstances are just as fraught and the interests just as high as in the 1950s and it seems likely that the law will continue to play a crucial role in this area.

Professor Duncan prefaces his comment on the case-law in this area, by remarking critically: 'The constitution has played a major role in adoption reform both by providing a basis for individual challenges to legislation, but also, paradoxically by imposing on the legislation something of a strait-jacket inhibiting or delaying the implementation of sometimes widely approved reforms.' [5] On the positive side, in *M v An Bord Uchtála* [1975] IR 1, the High Court struck down, as involving religious discrimination, a provision of the Adoption Act 1952. This provision (which, given the Hierarchy's outlook in 1952, had been a vital element in securing the Catholic Church's support for the introduction of adoption) stated that the adoptive parents had to be of the same religion as the child and his parents. The Court held that since this had the effect of preventing any adoption by spouses who were of different religions, it was discriminatory in its effect and hence unconstitutional on its face. And, in *O'G v Attorney General* [1985] ILRM 61, a widower was allowed to adopt a child placed with him before his wife's death, despite a ban on such an adoption in the Adoption Act 1974, because there was no equivalent in the case of a widow adopting a child: the judge held this ban to be an 'unwarranted denial of human equality' (at 68).

Elsewhere the judges' law-making has been less helpful. First of all, great emphasis has been given by the courts to the rights of the natural parents. The effect of this value judgement is to prefer their rights to those of the adoptive parents or even, more significantly, to those of the child, in circumstances in which it might seem preferable, from a neutral perspective, for the child to be brought up by the adoptive parents. Consider first a case in which it is the child of an unmarried mother who is being adopted. Her rights are based on nothing more than the 'unenumerated personal rights' (contained in Article 40.3.1). In other words, they are not dictated by any words of the Constitution but squarely constitute a judicial policy decision and a preference for the natural mother, possibly at the expense of the 'sanctity and security of the family resulting from adoption' (Henchy J., dissenting in the seminal case in this area, *M v Bord Uchtála* [1977] IR 287).

Another feature is that the father of a natural child is given no legal status in relation to the child. Under the legislation his consent to adoption is not required (save in very rare circumstances) and in *The State (Nicolaou) v An Bord Uchtála* [1966] IR 567, the Supreme Court held that this provision does not violate the right to gender equality since, in general, there is a significant difference in 'moral . . . capacity and social function' (Article 40.1) between the mother and father. Nor was the father even entitled to be heard by An Bord Uchtála (the Adoption Board) as to the fate of the child. The Court thereby put the applicant in *Nicolaou*, who was anxious to marry the mother and to care for the child, on a par, so far as legal rights are concerned, with a rapist. This attitude of the Irish courts was confirmed in *JK v VW* [1990] 2IR 437 (S.C.). However, on this occasion the father took his case to the European Court of Human Rights: in *Keegan v Ireland* [1994] 18EHRR 342, the European Court held that the father's rights under Article 6 of the European Convention (the family life provision) had been violated. Subsequently, An Bord Uchtála has modified its procedure to bring it into line with *Keegan*.[6]

Take next, the adoption of the child of a married couple. The relevant provision here is Article 41.1.1° which states: 'The State recognises the Family as the natural primary and fundamental unit group of Society, and as a moral institution possessing inalienable and imprescriptible rights, antecedent to all positive law.' Now it might have been thought that, in 1937 when there was some uncertainty as to how far judicial review of laws was part of the Constitution, this provision, whose phraseology is drawn from the Social Encyclicals of the 1920s and 30s, would have been regarded as merely a trumpet voluntary setting the scene for, and emphasizing the importance of, what follows. Instead, the Courts have fastened onto the phrase 'inalienable and imprescriptible' and assigned to it its full literal weight. The first situation in which it is relevant is where the sequence of events is as follows: first, an unmarried mother gives up her child for adoption; next, the mother marries the father so that she and her husband come within the scope of Article 43 and acquire the rights of a married couple. Finally, the newly married couple seek to recover the child from the adoptive parents. Apart from in the rather extreme circumstances considered below, the 'natural parents' will succeed because of the literal reading given by the judges to Article 41.1.1° and its reference to the 'inalienable and unprescriptible rights' of the family. This is so in spite of any psychological damage to the child.

Another result of this provision is that, with a narrow exception mentioned below, it has been held that any legislation purporting to enable *marital* children to be adopted would be unconstitutional, even where the married natural parents consent to adoption.[7] The outcome of this interpretation, in which very little weight was given to the rights of the child, is that up until the late 1980s thousands of marital children were condemned to live more or less unhappily in orphanages while, on the other side of the fence, there was an equivalent number of couples who were denied the opportunity to adopt. During this period successive Ministers for Justice had offered the judiciary's interpretation as a bar to bringing marital children within the haven of adoption. The legislature eventually took cautious action (caution which proved to be well-founded in the light of the interpretation offered in *Re Art. 26 and the Adoption (No. 2) Bill 1987* [1989] IR 656) in the form of the Adoption Act 1988. However the Act was cautious in that significant sets of restrictions were attached to its scope. The first is that the parents must 'for physical or moral reasons have failed in their duty towards the child'; it is likely that such failure will continue without interruption until the child is 18; and, finally, that 'such failure constitutes an abandonment [by the parents] of all parental rights'. This restrictive formulation is in part a quotation from Article 42.5 of the Constitution which creates an exception to Article 41.1.1°. It is (presumably) included because of the likelihood that, given the Court's earlier rulings, the new law would otherwise fail to pass constitutional muster. Moreover, even given this restrictive legislation, the courts' interpretation of it has been criticized. One commentator has remarked:

> The judgments delivered in *In re the Adoption (No. 2)* Bill 1987 [1989] IR 656] and *The Western Health Board v An Bord Uchtála* [1995] 3 IR 178 can be criticised for undue emphasis [on what a natural parent says and to the level of their resistance in litigation to a child being adopted] and for creating the possibility . . . of the courts refusing to free a child for adoption in all cases in which natural parents oppose their child being adopted, no matter how gross the failure in parental duty.[8]

The second major restriction is procedural but mighty important, namely that the meeting of all the necessary conditions must be 'shown to the satisfaction of the High Court'. In other words, the adoptive parents are required to undergo the trauma and delay of High Court proceedings. To explain the likely reason why this was thought to be necessary one needs to refer to another field of law. This is the Separation of Powers doctrine, dealt with in Chapter 8, which is a central feature of the Irish Constitution. One of the features of the doctrine which has been given most weight is that all aspects of the judicial function should be vested in a court, rather than, say, a tribunal, even an independent tribunal like An Bord Uchtála. The possibility that An Bord Uchtála was within the danger zone of the Separation of Powers arose from the way in which the judges have extended the scope of the doctrine (beyond its limits in the U.S.) to catch even functions which have traditionally been considered administrative in character rather than judicial. As a result, in the 1970s, the notion was very much abroad, and causing consternation among the 26,000 adoptive couples, that the adoption orders of their children might be held unconstitutional, by virtue of the Separation of Powers. The Government responded to this fear by promoting an amendment to the Constitution (in 1979) to exclude adoption orders from this danger.

However, to return to the adoption of marital children under the 1988 Act, there seems to have remained a lingering fear that matters to do with adoption might be judicial in character. And it does not seem to have occurred to anyone that the 1979 Amendment would have been broad enough to permit a body other than the High Court (say An Bord Uchtála) to make a finding that the natural parents had 'failed in their duty towards their children'; though it seems probable that it would in fact have done so. In any event the result of the judicial attitudes towards the 'inalienable and imprescriptible' formula and, secondly, to the Separation of Powers has been to permit the adoption of marital children only after a High Court hearing.

4. Social Reforming Legislation

This chapter adopts a different perspective from that normally taken by legal writers, who usually organize their material by reference to the particular constitutional rights that are violated by legislation the constitutionality of which is being challenged. Rather, our focus is mainly on the legislation under challenge itself – in this case, social reforming legislation – and also on whether it could have been brought within an exception to whatever constitutional right is involved. Social reforming legislation is law which is designed to help (broadly speaking) the poorer or weaker members of the community. Necessarily, this will usually be at the expense of the richer or stronger members of the community. The fate of legislation in constitutional challenges of this type will be discussed in Parts I-V of the chapter, under the heads of equality; trade unions; education; property rights, and joint tenancy for both spouses in the matrimonial home. In each, there is a curtailment of constitutionally-established individual rights, such as property, privacy, or the rights to carry on business or earn a livelihood. The corollary of this deprivation is that some advantage is given to a disadvantaged group. Sometimes it was sought to do this directly, as by altering rights between landlords and tenants or employers and employees. Sometimes the intention was to do it indirectly, by facilitating the State in helping a poorer or weaker section of the community. But whichever way the law is designed, where there is a constitutional challenge in marginal cases it is usually the established individual interest which the judges have preferred to the disadvantaged or to the community or collective interest, so that the law is struck down. We shall return to review this trend in Part VII, after we have described it, and, in part VI, discussed the judges' performance in the field of freedom of expression.

I Equality

To invoke the famous slogan of the French Revolution, one can say that the Irish judges have been very strong on *liberté*, but very weak on *egalité*, despite the fact that this value is explicit in Article 40.1 which states:

> All citizens shall, as human persons, be held equal before the law. This shall not be held to mean that the State shall not in its enactments have due regard to differences of capacity, physical and moral, and of social function.

In fact, '[the Courts] have given it [this provision] a restricted ambit'.[1] Now it is certainly understandable that the equality provision should not have been used positively by the courts to strike down laws. Such a usage would drag the courts more centrally into politics than any of the other provisions of the Constitution. But what might have been expected is that, when 'progressive' legislation enacted by the political organ in Leinster House is being assailed for violation of one of the conservative values in the Constitution (mentioned earlier), the equality provision should be used as a counterweight so as to protect the legislation from invalidation. In fact, because of the neglect of the equality provision, this has never been done.

One measure, which employed a number of classic social engineering devices to promote 'equality' and yet in which Article 40.1 was not drawn upon by the Court to defend the measure's constitutionality, was *Re Art. 26 and the Employment Equality Bill 1996* ([1997] 2 IR 321, in which this significant bill was held unconstitutional. Moreover, connected with it and consequently also biting the dust, was a similar measure, the Equal Status Bill 1996 ([1997] 2 IR 387).[2]

The Employment Equality Bill addressed all aspects of employment and unemployment conditions, including training, work experience and promotion. Its object was to outlaw discrimination whether arising from gender, marital status, sexual orientation, religion, age, disability, race or membership of the travelling community. The central ground on which the Employment Equality Bill failed was that in the case of disabled employees, it was for the employer to pay for any additional facilities that were necessary. Accordingly, the effect of the legislation was, the Court ruled, to 'transfer the cost of solving one of society's problems onto a particular group' (at p. 367) and it was held that this constituted an unjust attack on an employer's property right and right to earn his livelihood. However, this was not the first time that this type of issue had arisen and the draftsman had sought to anticipate and address it by providing (in s. 35) that where there was undue hardship, the cost of providing the 'additional facilities' would be met by the State. This statutory formula was defined widely to embrace the nature and cost of the facilities as well as 'the financial circumstances of the employer . . . [and] the disruption that would be caused by the . . . facilities'. Yet the Court brushed aside arguments founded on this provision, on the flimsy ground that operating it would mean that 'the employer would have to disclose his financial circumstances and the problems of his business to an outside party' (at p. 366). Since it has long been necessary for businesses to disclose such information for the purpose of (say) tax-assessment or grant allocation, this hardly seems adequate. Especially is this true when one recalls, as the Court had remarked earlier in the case: 'what is or is not required by the exigencies of the common good [the exception to the right which is permitted by the Constitution] is primarily [though not exclusively] a matter for the Oireachtas and this Court will be slow to interfere with the decision of the Oireachtas in this area' (at p. 367).

The other ground on which the Employment Equality Bill failed is that it created vicarious liability for the criminal offences (e.g. discrimination) that it established. Thus the employer is made liable for something done by his employees. Holding this to be unconstitutional, the Court stated (at pp. 373–74): 'The social policy of making the Act more effective does not, in the opinion of this Court, justify the introduction of so radical a change to our criminal law. The change appears to the Court to be quite disproportionate to the mischief with which the section seeks to deal'. This is the first occasion on which the device of proportionality has been used to strike down the substantive content of a criminal offence, as opposed to some evidential or procedural requirement. And one might query its use here. Given the difficulty, in a medium or large business, of finding out precisely who did discriminate, it makes sense to hold the employer responsible and thus to give him an incentive to put in place measures to prevent his employees from discriminating. There is no discussion of this type of practical consideration in the judgment.

The Court did moreover note that the technique of making an employer vicariously liable for the acts of his employees has long been used in the field of 'public welfare offences', e.g. offences established by public health law or consumer protection laws. However, while apparently accepting the constitutionality of such offences, the Court distinguished them from those established by the Bill before it, on the basis that the punishment in the 1996 Bill was more serious (a maximum of two years imprisonment and/or £15,000 fine) and, secondly, that it would 'attract a substantial measure of opprobrium'. But surely the levels of public disapproval – in other words disapproval in the eyes of the reasonable lay person – is unlikely to differ much from one type of regulatory offence to another. One might well feel that an ordinary lay person who was asked to classify theft, and offences under the 1996 Bill or (say) the Health and Safety at Work Regulations, would probably put the last two in the same category and theft in a separate and more serious category. And as regards the other part – the seriousness of the punishment – given the turnover of even medium-sized businesses, if the possibility of a staff fine were not available, then it would be realistic to expect the Bill to make no impact whatsoever.

II Trade Union Negotiating Rights

Another form taken by the tendency in favour of individual rights and against those of collective groups, to be found in the interpretation of the Constitution by the judges, concerns trade unions. This is evident in the muted expression given to the right to free association in the landmark case of *N.U.R. v Sullivan* (1947) IR 77. The substance of this case was an attack on the constitutionality of the Trade Union Act 1941. The history of this measure was unusual in that it was the outcome of a series of meetings between the Minister for Industry and Commerce, Mr Sean McEntee (not a politician known as a wide-eyed radical, and the General Secretary of the ITGWU, Mr William O'Brien. It was specifically designed to meet the situation of Irish trade unionism which – as Dr Irene Lynch remarks in a compelling analysis on which this section draws heavily – 'suffers from fragmented membership and inter-union competitiveness'.[3] The central provisions of the 1941 Act established a Trade Union Tribunal and stipulated that within each category of employment, only one particular union (determined by the Tribunal) would have the right to organize all others being excluded. The constitutionality of this provision was attacked by invoking the right to association (in Article 40.60 (iii)). The argument failed in the High Court because the legislation was held to come within the exception to the constitutional provision. However, writing for the Supreme Court, Murnaghan J. stated (at 102):

> The Constitution states the right of the citizens to form associations and unions in an emphatic way and it seems impossible to harmonise this language with a law which prohibits the forming of associations and unions and allows the citizens only to join prescribed associations and unions.

This crucial judgment takes a rather individualistic view of the right of association and in substance, this judgment delivers to the working man, so far as strong recognition rights are concerned, no bread rather than the half loaf offered by the 1941 Act. The net consequence is that, at a pivotal point in the development of modern industrial relations, an opportunity was missed.

In a survey of the judiciary's general performance, one must of course, recognize that *Sullivan* is now a venerable case. However, in a line of more recent authority which is similar to *Sullivan*, the courts have held that 'although the Constitution guarantees the right of an individual to join the union of his or her choice there is no corresponding obligation on the employer to recognize or bargain with that union'.[4] Cold comfort indeed.

III Education

For fifty plus years, the leading case in the field of secondary education was *Re Art. 26 and the School Attendance Bill* [1943] IR 334, 346 which also displays an anti-collectivist tendency, to no one's legitimate advantage. The Bill would have augmented the Minister for Education's powers to prescribe standards of education. The Bill was struck down on the basis that Article 42 of the Constitution establishes that normally the right and duty to provide for the education of children is vested in their parents. But Article 42 also states that 'the State shall . . . as guardian of the common good, require in view of actual conditions that the children receive a certain minimum education . . .' Yet this balancing provision did not carry the day for the State, largely because the Court ruled that it was confined to the standard of substantive education. By contrast, the central provision in the Bill catches 'not only the education, but also the manner in which each child is receiving it . . .' and empowers a Minister to fix standards in respect of each of these. This distinction has justifiably received poor press on the ground that content and manner of education are not separable in the way suggested.[5]

Whilst the case was decided several decades ago, its legacy haunts us yet. The governing legislation in this important and evolving area remains the School Attendance Act 1926. And, more generally, it remains a remarkable feature of the Irish schools system – often commented upon – that its administration is governed by hundreds of circulars and other non-legal instruments, rather than – as correct legal procedure requires – by acts of the Oireachtas or delegated legislation. It seems a reasonable guess that this phenomenon derives at least in part from the shock which the Department suffered in the early 1940s. However, the tide appears to have turned in *DPP v Best* [2000] 2 ILRM 1, which arose out of the prosecution of parents for failing to cause their children to attend national school, contrary to the 1926 Act. They pleaded not guilty on the basis of a defence authorized by the Act, namely that their children were receiving 'suitable elementary education' at home. One of the defence arguments relied upon a crucial passage from the *School Attendance Bill* reference which ruled that Article 42 should be interpreted in such a way that in applying the statutory defence, the teaching methods could not be taken into account, but simply the general subject matter. Keane J. (as he then was) expressly stated (at 33), and was probably implicitly supported by the other members of the majority, that this key aspect of the *School Attendance Bill* reference was wrong.

If this is now the law, it marks a significant change. It means that the sort of State regulation of school management that is considered within the State's power and indeed duty elsewhere, and that most lay persons assume is already the case here, the sort of regulation that was, for instance, contemplated in the abortive Green Paper *Education for a Changing World* (Pl 8969, 1992), could be implemented without fear that it would be struck down as soon as it suited any litigant to take the point.

IV Right to Property

The present area is often concerned with certain controls affecting the use or value of private property. As might be expected, therefore, the right to property looms very large. This right is established, indeed, in two separate provisions of the Constitution.[6] After a certain amount of fluidity in reconciling the two provisions the gist of the courts' approach has been that, while there is a right to property, it may be controlled by the law, provided that this is not 'unjust' (Article 40.3.2°) and is done in the interest of 'social justice' or 'the common good' (Article 43).

The right has been invoked but repulsed by the judges (rightly so, I believe) in a number of peripheral areas. Among these are the licensing and regulation of businesses; the powers to investigate the control of companies; and the freezing of bank accounts held by terrorist organizations. However, the point at which (as the Americans say) 'the rubber really hits the road' lies in the crucial areas in which there is some interference with private property in the interest of the wider community and the courts have to decide what meaning to give to the inevitably vague exceptions established by the Constitution property right. It is realistic to comment that there have been judicial mood swings, over time and among individual judges, as to how protective towards the private property right it is appropriate to be; and in consequence, how stringent towards legislation which interferes with it. We shall also notice how the judges' attitude has affected the choices available to the legislature and the Government in making law to protect (usually) the weaker members of society. The following analysis divides up cases according to whether a strongly pro-property or pro-community approach has been taken.

Pro-property approach

We may start by considering this question in the most frequently litigated area, land-use planning. On the one side is the right of the landowner to build what he wants on his own land and to use it for whatever purpose he wishes. On the other side is the interest of the community, whether in the form of the neighbours, passers-by or users of the environment.

Often the view has been taken judicially that planning control can only be constitutional if compensation is paid to the disappointed developer. The important point here is that it is usually the case that the value which land would have had if planning permission had been granted (which is the basis on which compensation is calculated) will depend upon developments surrounding the land, which have either been funded by public finance (e.g. roads, water supply or sewerage schemes) and/or are due to changes in society, such as population movement into an area which was formerly rural. Either type of change would, provided also that planning permission were granted, have the effect of substantially raising the value of land purchased at its agricultural value. Moreover – and here is the important point – each change will have come about without the would-be developer engaging himself in any expense or lifting a finger to bring about the change in value.

The (original) Local Government (Planning and Development) Act of 1963, gave land-owners refused planning permission a fairly strong entitlement to compensation from the local planning authority. Local authorities were, however, allowed an alternative to this payment, in that they could, instead of paying the developer compensation, give him an undertaking to grant permission for some different development in respect of the same land. While a rather small aggregate sum of money was paid (mainly by Dublin Corporation) in compensation, it is not known how many undertakings were given in order to avoid such payments. However, it is probable that they were numerous and that they led to the authorization of land for purposes which were not in the interests of the community or good planning.

A case which illustrates this system in operation and demonstrates, too, the majority judicial view that where there was neither compensation nor undertaking, the refusal of planning could often be unconstitutional is *Grange v Dublin County Council (No. 3)* [1989] IR 367, 375–76. Here the High Court upheld the validity of an undertaking (under the planning legislation). However, Murphy J. went on to warn that if the County Council's intention to grant permission in accordance with the undertaking given to the developer were to be frustrated because of objections by third parties (for instance, neighbours), then the Constitution would require that the County Council pay compensation.

A convergent line of authority has held that because of the constitutional right to property, even if the planning law need not be struck down, the statutory provisions as to compensation should, in the case of any ambiguity, be read in such a way as to maximize compensation. As McCarthy J. remarked in *Grange v Dublin Corporation* [1986] IR 246, 256: 'Since the Act of 1963 effects an interference with a personal right, it must be strictly construed: so much the more so, where the interference is being lessened . . . by compensation must any inclusion . . . of the right to compensation be, itself, so construed'.[7]

Against this background, it is striking, even perplexing, to notice another comment of McCarthy J. Giving the judgment of the Court in *XJS v Dun Laoghaire* [1986] IR 750, 753 (in which he, like the rest of the Court, found for the developer) he let drop the lapidary *dictum*:

> Assuming that the amount of the claim, £2,375,000, bears a real relationship to the award that may be made by the arbitrator, it will be seen that X.J.S. may anticipate a profit of over £2,000,000 on an investment of £40,000 in a period of 5 years. Such profit will be at the

> expense of the ratepayers of Dun Laoghaire. I allude to
> this alarming circumstance, not because of any argu-
> ment based thereon, but so as to direct attention to the
> question as to whether or not legislation which appears
> to authorise such a use of public funds is constitution-
> ally proper. On that question, I express no view.

This is an interesting remark. It is interesting because it is – so
far as I know – the only occasion on which a judge has even
suggested that any provision might be unconstitutional because
it leant too far in favour of the individual and not far enough in
support of that much-neglected group, the community. But I do
not think that the direction in which the suggestion (and it is
only a suggestion) points is a correct statement of law; and that
perhaps is why a judge not known for his reticence 'expressed
no view' and, indeed, why the developer won the case, despite
the remark. The reason is simply – and here is an important
omission – that the Constitution seldom lays down a *positive*
statement in favour of the State or community. The rights provisions are almost all in favour of the individual, though with
certain (negative) exceptions or limitations in favour of the State
or community. One or two limited areas apart, there is thus no
constitutional ban on the State over-paying an individual or
failing to levy a tax for a windfall profit.

To go back to the main train of thought – pro-property judgments – in an era in which the environment is at last being taken
seriously, one ought to notice Professor Casey's view (at p. 679):
'It is not clear, however, that some of the U.S. cases would have
been decided the same way in Ireland – e.g. *Miller v Schoene*
(1928) 276 U.S. 272, where legislation permitting the uncompen-
sated destruction of ornamental cedar trees to prevent cedar
rust from killing nearby apple orchards [the foundation of a
significant industry] was upheld.'

Turning next to the control of building-land prices, in the early
1970s, as in the 2000s, house prices were inflated by the huge
cost of building-land. This rise meant, on one side of the coin, a
huge disadvantage to first-time home-owners and, on the other,

frequent windfall profits to landowners who had bought land at agricultural prices (the same phenomenon that was noticed earlier in respect of planning permission). In 1973 a Committee chaired by Mr Justice Kenny which had been set up to advise the Minister for Local Government on this problem, reported.[8] Put briefly, its majority recommendation was that in 'designated areas' (in which the land had been increased in value by works carried out by the local authority) a local authority could acquire land compulsorily for house building.[9] The compensation payable would be based on its existing-use value, plus 25%, but – and here is the significant point – without regard to its development potential. The majority of the Committee considered that such a scheme would not violate the property right. However, in the years after the Kenny Report, the Courts decided a number of constitutional cases in which they took a strongly pro-property line and the Report was never implemented.

This is the sort of background that Dr Fitzgerald probably had in mind when he remarked: 'I can testify from personal experience in government that concern about possible restrictive interpretations of the Articles on private property has been a major impediment to legislation required in the public interest . . . for example in relation to the treatment of windfall profits from development land.'[10] One might add here that the dismal evidence of sleaze (not concerning governments led by Dr Fitzgerald) presently oozing from various Inquiries may suggest that certain politicians may not have been displeased to receive negative advice as regards what could be done to restrain various forms of property speculation. However, this does not alter the fact that a number of judgments gave a solid basis for such advice.

Commenting extra-judicially on this state of affairs, Keane J. (as he then was) remarked:

> The problem as I see it, is that any scheme which seeks to secure for the community the benefit of its investment in services may involve some element of expropriation without compensation. In the present

state of the authorities, it would be a rash person who
would predict the fate of such a scheme were it subjected to a constitutional challenge.[11]

The inspiration of the property right in the Irish Constitution is
generally supposed to be the encyclical *Quadragesimo Anno* by
Pope Pius XI (1931). The encyclical states that the institution of
private property is only justified so far as it is grounded in social
need. The judiciary has seldom looked back to this original
inspiration.

Two sets of comparisons also demonstrate the pro-property
tendency of some judges. The first of these is *Bhosphorus v
Minister for Transport* [1994] 2 ILRM 551, 559-60; [1996] 3 CMLR
257,[12] which arose when, acting under Serbian sanction regulations, the Minister impounded an aircraft because it was owned
by Yugoslavian Airlines, despite the fact that it had been leased
to a Turkish airline. The High Court (at 559-60) held that this
action was invalid as being 'a wholly unwarranted intervention
in the business of [the Turkish Airline]'. This decision was in
effect reversed by the European Court of Justice on the ground
that the impounding was justified by the 'objective of . . . putting
an end to the state of war . . . and to the massive violations of
human rights . . . in the Republic of Bosnia-Herzegovina' ([1996]
3 CMLR at 295). The same broad point – the stronger preference
of the Irish, than of the EU, judiciary, for the rights to property or
to run a business – may be illustrated by reference to the judgment of the European Court of Justice and the subsequent
decision of the Supreme Court in *Duff v Minister of Agriculture &
Food* [1996] ECR 1-535; [1997] 2 IR22. In this case the plaintiffs,
who were development farmers, challenged the validity of a
decision of the Minister not to allocate them milk quotas. The
Court of Justice ruled that the Minister, *as a matter of Community
law*, had not infringed principles of legitimate expectations.
Somewhat surprisingly, a majority of the Supreme Court applied
national law principles of legitimate expectations to the case at
hand and concluded that the manner in which Minister had

exercised his discretion infringed these national law principles.

Pro community-interest authorities

We may start this summary of the divergent line of cases with the leading authority of *Re Art. 26 and Part V of the Planning and Development Bill 1999* [2000] 2 IR 321. The statutory scheme set up by the Bill envisaged that a landowner who developed his property for housing and who was not exempted by other provisions of Part V would in general be required to cede up to twenty per cent of the land to the housing authority for the provision of houses for poorer members of the community. The price to be paid for this piece of land would be based on the existing use of the land (normal agricultural value) and would, accordingly, be significantly below the market value of the land, (if by market value is meant the price which the property might have been expected to fetch if sold on the open market, with a right to develop). Compensation would accordingly be paid for the undoubted restriction on the exercise by the landowner of his property rights, but it would be at an amount significantly short of its market value.

The Court commenced its analysis by stating that where property is compulsorily acquired by the State for social objectives, the owner is usually entitled to compensation at market value. But it continued with the key assumption that (at p. 353):

> [A land-owner holds land] . . . subject to any restrictions which the general law of planning imposes on the use of the property in the public interest. Inevitably, the fact that permission for a particular type of development may not be available for the land will, in certain circumstances, depreciate the value in the open market of that land. Conversely, where the person obtains a permission for a particular development the value of the land in the open market may be enhanced.

Keane J. then went on to quote from *Pine Valley v Minister for the Environment* [1987] IR 23 the observation:

> That purchase of land for development purposes is manifestly a major example of a speculative or risk

> commercial enterprise. Changes in market values or economic forces, *changes in decisions of planning authorities and the rescission of them* . . . may make the land more or less valuable. (Italics in original).

Keane J. also cited *Central Dublin v AG* 109 I.L.T.R. 69 [1975] in which restrictions on the statutory right to demand compensation for the refusal of planning permission did not make the planning system unconstitutional. And he might also have noted that post-*Central Dublin* amendments of the Planning Code further restricting the right to compensation have not been subjected to constitutional challenge. Against this background, the Court characterized the 2000 Bill in this way (at p. 63):

> In the present case, as a condition of obtaining a planning permission for the development of lands for residential purposes, the owner may be required to cede some part of the enhanced value of the land, deriving both from its zoning for residential purposes and the grant of permission, in order to meet what is considered by the Oireachtas to be a desirable social objective, namely the provision of affordable housing and housing for persons in the special categories and of integrated housing.

While the reasoning is not entirely clear, it seems that this characterization is the key point and that the conclusion that the Bill was constitutional then followed irresistibly. But it is well to emphasize that the key assumption on which the decision was erected was the view that the value of the land in respect of which the owner has a constitutional right is not necessarily its (enhanced) value with planning permission. Once this point is conceded, then it follows that what is in effect a rough and ready levy, in exchange for the extra value bestowed by the planning permission, is acceptable.

While many may regard this key holding as an eminently reasonable view, the simple point being made here is that there have been a number of other judges (described in the earlier section) who have not taken this view.

Another line of cases in accord with the tenor of the Article 26 reference just summarized, are the cases holding that taxi licences are not to be regarded as property rights and, consequently, that if fresh licences are created, compensation need not be paid to existing licence-holders, whose licences have thereby been devalued: *Hempenstall v Minister for the Environment* [1993] ILRM 318; *Humphrey v Minister for the Environment* High Court, 13 October 2000. The preference shown in *Humphrey* for what may be thought of as the community interest over against a strong view of property rights, may be illustrated by the following extract from the case: 'a quantitative restriction not alone affects the rights of citizens to work in an industry for which they may be qualified but it also manifestly affects the *right of the public to the services of taxis* and, indeed, restricts the development of the taxi industry itself' (my emphasis). The taxi licence cases may also be regarded as an illustration of the notion that the courts should operate an especially rigorous review against the decisions of a public authority, if it is suspected that these decisions have been taken at the behest of some pressure group.

V Joint Ownership of Matrimonial Home

In *L v L* [1982] ILRM 115, 120, Finlay C.J. remarked:

> . . . anything that would help to encourage the basis of full sharing in property values as well as in every other way between the partners of a marriage, must directly contribute to the stability of the marriage, the institution of the family and the common good.

This encomium naturally prompted a commentator to remark that 'any doubts that may have existed about possible constitutional difficulties [regarding joint ownership of the matrimonial home] seem to have been set at rest by the Supreme Court's attitude . . . '[13] However, the Court sounded a different note in *Re Article 26 and the Matrimonial Home Bill 1993* [1994] ILRM 241.

Subject to an exception considered below, this Bill would have applied automatic ownership as joint tenants of the matrimonial home to both spouses. The Court ruled that the Bill was unconstitutional in that it is for the married couple themselves to decide as to the ownership of their home and any interference with this right would constitute a violation of Article 41.1.1° which is the Article that guarantees the authority of the family. Now, the draftsman had anticipated the Court's line of criticism and had provided for an exception, namely that the Bill should not apply if the non-owning spouse were to declare in writing that, after taking legal advice, s/he did not wish the measure to apply. But the Court was not satisfied with this since the non-owner might refuse to make the declaration and, even if this refusal were unreasonable, the owner spouse could restore his or her sole ownership only by taking High Court proceedings. In the present instance[14] the Court chose to regard this as a very high hurdle to jump.

Ultimately, what underpins the Court's judgment is its assumption that, at the time at which the matrimonial home was acquired, the parties had taken a 'free and full' decision about the legal status of their house. In the circumstances of most couples, this seems to be a most unrealistic assumption (on which no evidence was laid before the Court). Accordingly, the Court's first thoughts on this matter (voiced in *L* and quoted earlier) might seem to be closer to common experience and common sense.

VI Freedom of Expression and Reform

Here there is a break with previous parts in this chapter in that we are not concerned with social reform legislation and the Courts' use of the Constitution at the behest of litigants who wish legislation to be struck down. Rather, we are concerned with the Courts' failure to use the Constitution to reform possibly out of date common law rules and we are confining our comments to a single area of the Constitution, which is concerned with free speech and the transfer of information. (The exact formulation in Article 40.6.1° is 'the right of the citizens to express freely their convictions and opinions'. But nothing significant turns on the language of the provision.) However, what this part does have in common with the rest of this chapter is that it is concerned with the same contest between individual and community interests, in this case, reputation versus free speech and the free circulation of information.

Defamation

Defamation originated in the Court of the Star Chamber, in the heyday of absolute monarchy. Reflecting its origin, this law possesses a number of features which are out of line with the rest of the common law and which give the plaintiff a substantial advantage. Thus to take a few examples: the plaintiff does not have to establish that the defendant was negligent or to show that he has suffered any concrete loss (e.g. failure to secure promotion or loss of profit in a business), nor is it a defence that the plaintiff failed to object to an earlier publication of the same material.

The need for some reform seems plain. The tool might seem to lie readily to hand, namely drawing up a better balance between the two divergent constitutional rights: protection of a right to one's good name (Article 40.3.2°) and, on the other hand, the (overlapping) rights of free communication and expression (Articles 40.3.1° and 40.6.1.i). And sure enough reform has come through the Constitution in the U.S., Australia and Canada. Even in pre-Human Rights Act Britain, there was progress.

But not in Ireland. *De Rossa v Independent Newspapers*[15] arose out of an allegation made by a newspaper regarding various deeds that had been done during the evolution of the party, which had, by the time of the newspaper article, become Democratic Left. The action was brought by the Leader of the Party. This might be thought just the sort of situation in which some alleviation of the libel law might have been justified for it involved material of legitimate public interest, something which it was peculiarly difficult for the newspaper to prove. A High Court jury awarded damages of £300,000 (three times the previous highest award). On appeal to the Supreme Court, it was accepted that the Constitution required that there should be proportionality between the wrong done to the defendant's reputation and the size of the award. But, given the rather nebulous nature of proportionality and the inevitable inexperience of a jury in assessing the highly subjective issue of damage to reputation, this reference to proportionality seems to amount to much ado about nothing. This is especially so because of the majority holding that no numerical guidance could be given to the jury as to the upper and lower bounds of the award. The result is that the only remote rock of predictability in the system remains an appeal to the Supreme Court. But, given the menace of costs, this is an infrequent recourse. Nor was there any support in *De Rossa* for the principle established by the European Court of Human Rights, that plaintiffs who are public figures ought to be treated differently from those who are not.[16] The case has now been referred to the European Court (where it seems likely to be – in effect – reversed).

Law of Confidence

However, as against this, there are recent authorities in which the freedom of expression has been used rather expansively, according to Dr Quinn, 'to create breathing space for the media to access information and to publish it [since otherwise] the quality of the democratic process is in some doubt.'[17] The first of these authorities is especially comparable with the libel authorities. It is *National Irish Bank v RTE* [1998] 2 ILRM 233 – which arose when RTE obtained internal documents which were relevant to allegations about improper offshore bank accounts. The Bank sought an injunction to restrain the broadcasting of this material. Relying in part on the Article relating to freedom of expression in the Constitution, the Supreme Court expanded the 'public interest' exception in the common law of confidence and ruled against the Bank.

Court trials

The second case, *Irish Times v Murphy* [1998] 1 IR 359, involved the Supreme Court in making a choice between free speech and its own traditional interest in a fair trial. The trial was a high-profile drug prosecution in respect of which the Circuit Court judge had felt it necessary to apply stringent restrictions on media reportage. The Court lifted these restrictions. Admittedly, it did so on the particular facts of the case, but it was also influenced by the notion of the community's interest in free reportage of court proceedings. However, a somewhat different note was struck in *Kelly v O'Neill* [2000] ILRM 108. This case arose out of an attempt to prosecute a journalist for contempt of court on the basis of an article critical of the accused, published – and here is the important point – after conviction but before sentence. The Supreme Court refused to rule that there were no circumstances in which an article published during this period would amount to a contempt.

A related matter concerns the Article 34.1 rule that justice must be administered 'in public . . . save in such special and limited cases as may be prescribed by law'. In a long line of authority,[19] the balance built into this provision has been interpreted rather strongly in the direction of court hearings 'in the sunshine' with claims for private hearings being frequently rejected.

VII Concluding Comment

Pursuing one of the main themes of this pamphlet, we have been concerned in this chapter with the competition between community and individual interests. We have considered how the tension between these interests have been resolved in four areas – equality, education, property, and joint ownership of the matrimonial home. The form which this tension has taken are laws authorizing the State to interfere on behalf of a weaker party with established individual interests. In each, as we have seen, the established individual interest has usually triumphed. However, just recently, leading Supreme Court decisions have taken a significant turn in favour of the community, in the fields of education and property. In a fifth area, trade union negotiation rights, the collective interest is represented by the trade union rather than the State, and it is a union's right to exclusive bargaining authority which is counterpoised against the right of the individual employee to join the union of his or her choice (however ineffectual a union which does not enjoy exclusive rights may prove to be). Again, the individual interest won and the community lost. Part VI dealt with the judges' refusal to use the right of free speech given in the Constitution to reform the law of libel because of the weight given to the protection of the individual's reputation. But in contrast, there are the cases in two other areas in which constructive use was made of the right of free speech to implement the public's right to know.

I must emphasize that in each of these areas, I have selected – and deliberately so – 'marginal cases', i.e. cases in which the conflicting considerations have seemed to be evenly balanced. What is striking is how often the individual interest has prevailed, and the community has lost.

All this may seem quite innocuous, so long as one thinks in terms like 'State' or 'collectivist' with their overtones of apathetic and anonymous 'bureaucrats' (than which no term is more pejorative). However, in reality it is the State which represents the community in its legal form and, apart from the occasional act of family duty or charity, it is substantially the State which succours the sick, the needy or the aged and guards against catastrophes to the community. Thus, to take a dramatic example of the competing interests hat may be at stake: on one side of the coin may be a tragedy on the scale of the Stardust discotheque fire, waiting to happen because of the legal difficulty in devising and enforcing an effective safety control system. On the obverse side of the coin may be a business person's property and privacy rights and the right to do business, supplemented by zealous protection of an accused's rights which are applied even where it is the funds of a corporation, rather than the liberty of an individual, which is at stake.

In the next chapter, we shall see how the same tension – between collective and individual rights – has been played out, with similar results, in the context of public inquiries.

Another type of situation, involving to some degree similar issues, arises where what was at stake was the constitutionality of a taxation law or large-scale State expenditure. In this situation, as we shall see in Chapter 6, the Courts have been somewhat more sensitive to the rights of the community.

5. Public Inquiries: The People's Right to Know

In the 1990s, there have been several episodes of suspected dishonesty, incompetence or failure of openness and account-ability in the fields of politics and the public service or big business which have given rise to substantial public and media disquiet. During the (present) 'era of tribunals' which began with the so-called Beef Tribunal (1991–94), we have had about a dozen inquiries (in one form or other) into such matters of public interest. Indeed, it could almost be said that these inquiries have become a part of the conventional constitution, despite not being mentioned in the *Bunreacht*. It would be possible to write a history of Ireland in the 1990s, centring upon their subject matter. Typically, what happens is that some pillar of the State or business – the beef industry, the Blood Transfusion Service Board, Cabinet Ministers, the planning system, the Revenue Commissioners, AIB – appears to have misbehaved. Often matters are exacerbated because the designated State watchdog has failed to bark. Usually, politicians are involved because, in our much-governed State, politicians are involved in everything, bad or good (though the latter is often forgotten). To assuage public concern, a public inquiry[1] is set up. Downstream, legal sanctions, either in the criminal or the civil field, might seem to beckon; yet somehow they are never reached. The point is that inquiries are essential machinery in implementing the public right to know about government and big business.

While public inquiries can take many forms, the Rolls Royce among inquiries is grounded on the Tribunals of Inquiry (Evidence) Act 1921–98 and, by inveterate convention (because of the general respect in which judges are held), an inquiry under this legislation is always chaired by a (serving or retired) senior judge. However, our concern here is not with the form of the inquiry but with the way in which the conduct and decisions of inquiries have been treated, where, as they often have been, they are brought before the High (or Supreme) Court for judicial review. In particular I wish to continue the broad inquiry launched in the previous chapter by examining a few selected cases from the perspective of the tension between the community interest in the effective and timely conduct of the inquiry versus the individual interest in privacy, reputation, strict procedure or the payment of party's legal costs out of public funds. Given the space available, I shall focus on five cases, chosen for their importance and because the issues were closely balanced. This last factor – that the issue was well-balanced – is worth emphasizing. For, here, as elsewhere in this book, I am not concerned with indisputable decisions (whether for or against the community). What the cases seem to show is that a strongly pro-individualistic slant took a turn in favour of the community in the fifth case, decided by the Keane Court.

Strictly speaking, the first case to be treated here involved an *obiter dictum*, but one which has had immense consequences. The starting point is the relevant legislation, which, as it was at the time, stated: 'Where a tribunal . . . is of the opinion that, having regard to the findings of the tribunal . . . there are sufficient reasons rendering it equitable to do so, the tribunal may direct that one person may pay another's costs' (Tribunals of Inquiry (Evidence)(Amendment) Act 1979, s.6). Despite these 'plain words', McCarthy J. remarked in *Goodman International v Hamilton (No. 1)* [1992] 2 IR 542, 605 that 'the liability to pay costs cannot depend upon the findings of the tribunal as to the subject matter of the inquiry.'

Why not? No reason is stated in the judgment but the reasoning may have been – it may be conjectured – that since the State (by way of the Oireachtas) had set up the tribunal, it should be responsible for any legal costs which flow from it. In other words since the State had willed the end, the State must will the means. But, one might reply, the State does not set up a tribunal as an act of wilfulness, but rather as a legitimate and predictable response to some suspected act of misconduct. If it turns out that a party is indeed found by the tribunal to have committed such an act, why should the party not bear the legal costs, if it chooses to be legally represented before the tribunal? And, anyway, apart from this sort of policy argumentation, the words of the relevant provision quoted earlier ('[if] there are sufficient reasons') are perfectly clear. To have re-written them went well beyond a judge's proper role.

Nevertheless the Beef Tribunal cited McCarthy J.'s *dictum* as one of its main grounds for ordering the State to pay the massive bill of costs for almost all parties at the Beef Tribunal. This totalled about £18 million (and, of course higher figures are often quoted in the media: a lie is often halfway round the world before the truth can get its boots on). And this bill for costs was – to politicians and public – among the most significant aspects of the Beef Tribunal. It made judicial inquiries (at any rate, until the Hepatitis C Tribunal of 1996–97) hugely unpopular and it meant that in three episodes where they would have been appropriate, other types of (non-judicial) inquiry were attempted, the outcomes from which duly proved unsatisfactory.[2]

Secondly, the question of the correct observance of constitutional justice (fair procedure) by inquiries has generated several applications for judicial review. Many of these involve merely the straightforward implementation of existing rules. But here we consider a case in which there was a finely balanced choice to be made by the court. *Haughey v Moriarty* [1999] 3 IR 1 grew out of the Tribunal of Inquiry into the financial affairs of a man who had been Taoiseach on four occasions and who, it was alleged, had received substantial payments from a business source. The Tribunal had made orders for production of documents, including the bank accounts of Mr Haughey and members of his family. The ruling of the Supreme Court was that the tribunal should have given notice to the persons affected by the orders and allowed them the opportunity to make representations objecting to disclosure.

The Court's ruling was presented as a straightforward application of the second rule of constitutional justice ('hear the other side'). But this still leaves the question of whether the rule should have been applied at this stage at all. Three points are relevant here. First, the primary focus of these tribunals is the public interest in ascertaining fully what happened and one would expect the courts – in setting the balance between the interest of a private individual and the community interest – to take this basic point into account.

In the second place, and even more important in this context, there is a further point of difference from court proceedings, namely that in a court the person seeking discovery would be an adversary, whereas in the case of a tribunal, the agency doing so is a neutral body constituted to investigate the facts impartially, whose chairperson – and this is an important point – is a High Court judge. Thirdly, it bears emphasis that constitutional justice is certainly involved at the stage of the oral hearings of a tribunal. Why then is it necessary for it also to be involved at the preliminary stage? For until the stage of the oral hearing, the documents will remain confidential to the staff of the tribunal. One may summarize these three criticisms by saying that, in *Haughey*, the Supreme Court appears to have simply applied to the Tribunal, the same procedure as regards discovery as if it were a court.

However, in this as in other areas, the Keane Supreme Court has sounded a different note. This was so, I believe, in the third case to be considered here, *Lawlor v Flood* Supreme Court, 24 November 2000. Here the applicant argued that he was entitled to give evidence in private before the Flood Tribunal. Keane C.J. stated that:

> [A Tribunal] would, of necessity, hear some matters in private as it assembled evidence. Certain aspects might

be conducted in private for the obvious reason that it might otherwise lead to unsubstantiated or irrelevant allegations being given widespread currency. But a tribunal could at some stage come to a decision that the evidence of particular persons be heard in public and that was the stage matters had reached in Mr Lawlor's case.

More generally, Keane C.J. remarked that: 'the courts, when interpreting legislation, must accord a significant measure of discretion to a tribunal about the manner in which it conducted proceedings.' The case indicates a strengthening in the position of the tribunal as against the individuals whose conduct is under investigation and this line has been followed in a number of recent cases.

Rather clearly in each of these three cases, there was a contest between the interest of the community (in the form of the inquiry) and that of the individual. In the remaining two cases, unusually, the tension was between the community and State institutions. The first of these is the so-called 'Cabinet Confidentiality' case (*A.G. v Hamilton (No. 1)* [1993] 2 IR 250). Here the Attorney General successfully challenged the Beef Tribunal's right to question a former Minister about whether a particular decision (to allocate the lion's share of the Government-sponsored export credit guarantee to a single meat exporter) had actually been brought before a Government meeting. In the High Court, O'Hanlon J. had upheld this line of questioning, remarking pointedly: 'I do not consider that our Constitution has failed to protect the public interest in the manner suggested. It would hardly be a model of its kind if it were so deficient'. But his decision was reversed in the Supreme Court. The central constitutional provision, on which the majority ruling rested, stated simply that the Government's responsibility to the Dáil was 'collective' and it was mainly from this that the obligation of absolute responsibility was deduced. This is a remarkable example of literal interpretation (on which see pp. 93–7). What is striking is that such a conclusion was drawn in the extreme circumstances of the Beef Tribunal, which had been designed to allay public disquiet by investigating this very issue. Moreover, they did so in face of opposing precedents from Britain and Australia, to the effect that the obligation of confidentiality is qualified by reference to countervailing factors, like the time which has passed since the period under scrutiny or the importance of the inquiry's work. At the very least, though, it must be said that here the Supreme Court was not afraid to risk public unpopularity. There was certainly ample criticism and within a few years the ruling was reversed by constitutional amendment (Seventeenth Amendment of the Constitution Act 1997).

Finally, take *A.G. v Hamilton* (No. 2) [1993] ILRM 821 which arose when, at the Beef Tribunal, counsel for Goodman International sought to cross-examine certain Dáil deputies as to the identity of the sources for the allegations that they had made against the company. The Supreme Court held that to allow this line of cross-examination would be to violate parliamentary privilege (as established in Article 15.12). Blayney J. stated (at 830): 'The reason why the [deputies] cannot be compelled to reveal the sources of their allegations is because those allegations are identical with the utterances in the Dáil and so they would be denied the immunity to which they are entitled in respect of the latter.'

If one takes the purposive attitude to interpretation – specifically, here, that the object of parliamentary privilege is to ensure that deputies are free to represent the interest of constituents in the Dáil without fear of being called before a court – there is much to be said for this result. On the other hand, such an attitude is in marked contrast with the literal perspective which had carried the day in the 'Cabinet Confidentiality' case. In addition, this result does involve an expansionist interpretation for the reason that what was at issue was whether the privilege extended to the repetition outside the Dáil, of utterances made in the Dáil; whereas the wording of Article 15.12 refers to 'utterances made in either House'. Yet the few other court decisions on parliamentary privilege have been remarkable for both the narrow scope given to it and the wide powers of supervision over proceedings in the Oireachtas which the courts have allowed themselves.[3]

What these two cases have in common is that in each scant help was available to the Court from the conventional legal guidelines of either the constitutional provisions (which were too general to be of assistance) or past precedents (non-existent). Accordingly, the Supreme Court had to make its decision in part by reference to 'the merits'. In each case, it decided that the integrity of a central institution of State (the Government in the 'Cabinet Confidentiality' case; the Dáil, in particular a deputy's relations with a constituent, in *Hamilton (No. 2)*) was to be preferred to the effective operation of the Beef Tribunal. Earlier, in close cases, we have analysed the 'winners and losers', by reference on one hand to the State (or community) and on the other hand, the individual. The present situation is unusual in that the tension was between the organs of State and the community interest in information. In these cases – in which no individual interest was involved – it was the organs of State which triumphed and the community interest in information which was defeated.

One of the general themes of this pamphlet – namely, the judiciary's failure to build a strong principle of community interest – is of interest in the present context. The issue is straightforward. These public inquiries were set up with a single major purpose: to ascertain and to inform the public about the truth of certain episodes that were of legitimate interest to them. There was no other purpose; for instance, the tribunals have not (save in a very few insignificant cases) led on to criminal prosecutions or civil proceedings. Yet in four of the five marginal cases surveyed, it is the strong community interest in the right to be informed about government and big business which has had to take second place. The exception is the most recent case of *Lawlor*, decided by the present Keane Supreme Court, which seems to be part of a more pro-Inquiry trend.

Despite *Lawlor*, one might risk a prediction about a query

which very naturally arises here: is there any basis on which to demand a court order directing a tribunal to allow itself to be the subject of live broadcast, so that all citizens have the chance to hear its proceedings? As far as statute law goes, the answer is that the chairman of each tribunal is empowered to decide on the tribunal's procedure and this includes the important question of broadcasting. And in the case of at least one tribunal, the chairman has ruled against a request to allow broadcasting. The central question, for present purposes, is whether such a refusal could be challenged on constitutional grounds. This seems most unlikely. In the first place, the Constitution naturally contains nothing specific on tribunals of Inquiry nor any general doctrine on openness or the accountability of public institutions and representatives and no implied doctrine in this field has been developed by the judiciary. It seems almost certain, therefore, that in respect of broadcasting, as in many of the other areas surveyed, the community's right to know would lose out again.

6. Taxation and Large-Scale Public Expenditure

The involvement of the courts in the areas of taxation and large-scale public expenditure is a novelty. The conventional wisdom was that it is the forte of the courts to deal with such areas as pre-trial criminal rights, including control over the powers of search and arrest; fair procedure in administrative agencies; and other civil rights. By contrast, the areas involving major public expenditure and taxation were, for a number of reasons, regarded as most appropriately dealt with by the political organs. In the first place, broad-based public issues in this area always depend upon fundamental choices. Most people would accept that public expenditure on health, education, overseas aid or (probably) better roads is a good thing; also and possibly more so, that reduction of taxes is good. But in the real world, where resources are limited, we cannot have all these good things; we have to choose. Who is to order priorities? The usual answer is: the Government or the Oireachtas. It is legitimate for ministers and deputies to do this because it is for the elected representatives of the people to decide on major questions of public expenditure or taxation. Readers will recall the great slogan of the American Revolution: 'No taxation without representation!' There is, secondly, the practical feature that ministers are advised by a cadre of expert, experienced civil servants. By contrast, judges are totally without advisers, indeed must, as a constitutional matter, be alone and independent. Moreover, the place and procedure within which judges must take their decisions are peculiarly ill-designed as forums for decisions of this type. The focus of a court is naturally upon the individual litigants who are before it. The contest between the plaintiff (sometimes carefully selected, just because s/he amounts to an especially hard case) and the defendant before the court is not designed to bring out the general context and ramifications of the decision. Thus shrouded from the court's gaze are the different circumstances of persons not before the court; the pros and cons of alternative choices to the measure whose constitutionality is at issue; and the knock-on effects of any court case. Yet these matters are the very stuff of socio-economic policy-making.

I Taxation Cases

The truth of the conventional wisdom that the courts should usually avoid striking down taxation legislation has been recognized in a number of judicial statements. One instance is *Madigan v Attorney General* [1986] ILRM 123, 45 (an unsuccessful challenge to the constitutionality of residential property tax) in which O'Hanlon J. remarked that the plaintiff in such a case 'faces a very uphill battle . . . [T]ax laws are in a category of their own and very considerable latitude must be allowed to the legislature in the enormously complex task of organising and directing the financial affairs of the state.'

Yet, in fact, a few of the constitutional challenges to a tax law have succeeded. The earliest and probably the most far-reaching is the Supreme Court decision (by 3:2 majority) in *Murphy v AG* [1982] IR 241, which held (as had German and Italian constitutional courts earlier) that it was unconstitutional for each spouse not to have a set of taxation allowances each, in the same way as would two single people. This feature, it was held, violated Article 41.3.1° in which the State promises 'to guard with special care the institution of Marriage on which the Family is founded and to protect it against attack.'

Three comments should be made. The first of these concerns the fact that Article 41.2 states that: '. . . by her life, within the home, woman gives to the State a support without which the common good cannot be achieved. The State shall, therefore endeavour to ensure that Mothers shall not be obliged by economic necessity to engage in labour to the neglect of their duties.' One way of interpreting this provision would have been to hold that, taken as a whole, (the family) Article 41 should not be read as requiring the taxation system to be adjusted so as to encourage women to work outside the home. There are, possibly, counters to this line of argument, notably that the case should be regarded as a strong implementation of the doctrine that the Constitution should be read by the contemporary standards as these vary from decade to decade and not by the standards of 1937 (as Walsh J. remarked in *McGee*, '. . . the constitution is 'speaking always in the present tense'). And yet, for the judgments to make no reference to counsel's arguments, which, as can be imagined, did rely on the plain wording of Article 41.2, is at the least very poor judge-craft, especially considering the respect paid elsewhere to the literal interpretation of the Constitution (on which see pp. 93-7).

The second point is that the State's laws and other actions will necessarily interact with named couples, for good or ill, at a number of points. These are so designed that at some points – and counsel for the State naturally gave examples of these – they will discriminate in favour of a married couple, as compared with an unmarried couple. At other points – of which the law before the court was the leading example – the reverse will be the case. The issue here, therefore, is whether the State could defend itself by submitting that on balance (so far as State involvement through tax, welfare benefits, etc. is concerned) the advantages conferred by the State on a married couple outweighed the disadvantages; or whether the law now requires that the married couple must be favoured at every point. This unreasonable suggestion seems to have been rejected. The Court appeared to accept the notion of a balance; but to hold that, in the circumstances, no balance of advantage in favour of a married couple had been made out. However, drawing up such a balance entails a somewhat subjective appreciation of various advantages and disadvantages (which may vary from time to time even in the same marriage, not to mention from one marriage to another).[1]

The third comment is that at a time of grave deterioration in the public finances (the first half of the 1980s), the decision caused a substantial increase in the tax burden falling on single persons. The political and economic implications of this were naturally not considered in the judgment. The conventional legal retort to a mention of this factor is of course to say that a court cannot and should not be concerned with such factors; the phrase *fiat iustitiae ruat coelum* ('let justice be done, though the Heavens fall') may even spring to the lips. But this rather misses the point of the line of criticism here, which is that the usual reason why a court need not consider the context and wider ramifications of its decisions is that normally its decisions are within a small enough compass for the ramifications to be negligible. Where this is not so, two alternatives are possible, neither of which is appropriate. The first would be for the court to ignore the wider ramifications, despite their relevance. The other would be for a court to attempt to take into account these wider ramifications, something which it has neither competence nor authority to do. The only way to avoid this fork is to adhere to the conventional eschewal of striking down taxation measures, save in extreme cases.

What may be regarded as the extreme case materialized in *Daly v Revenue Commissioners* [1995] 3 IR 1. Here the constitutionality of income tax withholding measures, established by the Finance Act 1990 was condemned by the High Court (Costello J.). This case differs from *Murphy* in that it did not amount to a root and branch disapproval of the tax. Rather, the judgment was grounded on the principle of proportionality, the basis of which is that the predicate of the objective, established by the legislature, is accepted and the court focuses its attention on the issue of whether the infringement of the tax-payer's right is out of proportion to the objective sought by the legislature. However, there is another broad feature which the case shared at least with *Murphy*. The tax struck down in *Daly* affected the self-employed. This was a group which, notoriously, had not contributed their fair share to income tax revenue in the 1970s and 80s. Seen in this light, the tax law before the court in *Daly* was designed to achieve a substantial measure of catching up. This kind of 'group justice' argument was, of course, one which could not be considered by the High Court, which could only take into account whether the tax law before it infringed the particular plaintiff's rights. And this sort of limitation is one of the principal reasons why courts are wisest to avoid the area of the constitutionality of tax law.

There is a further point of general application, which is, however, especially likely to arise in the tax field. It may be the case that the challenger's circumstances are such that he suffers from the fact that the infringement of his rights is out of proportion to the objective sought by the legislature. Yet the striking down of the law will often profit many other people whose circumstances are such that they would have fallen within the scope of the law, even if it had been constitutionally designed.

II Public Expenditure Cases

Three sets of cases are relevant here. Take first the High Court case of *O'Reilly v Limerick* [1989] ILRM 181 in which Costello J.

rejected the plaintiff traveller's claim (founded alternatively on Article 40.3 or 41.2) that he had a constitutional right to be provided with certain resources, specifically a halting site. The plaintiff's argument, according to Costello J., entailed the proposition that there has been a failure to distribute adequately in the plaintiff's favour a portion of the community's wealth. Costello J. drew a distinction between distributive justice (the distribution and allocation of common goods and common burdens) and commutative justice (fixing what is due to one individual from another individual). He classified the instant claim as involving distributive justice and concluded (at 195):

> I am sure that the concept of justice which is to be found in the Constitution embraces the concept that the nation's wealth should be justly distributed (that is the concept of distributive justice), but I am equally sure that a claim that this has not occurred should, to comply with the Constitution, be advanced in Leinster House rather than in the Four Courts.

Secondly, consider *Brady v Cavan County Council* [2000]1ILRM 81. Here the applicant had claimed an order against the respondent local authority requiring it to keep the roads in its care in an adequate condition, despite the plea that to do so would leave the defendant with inadequate funds to discharge their duties in other areas, such as public housing or water or sewerage facilities. The Supreme Court rejected this claim by a majority, resting its decision on the basis that the defendant did not have the means to comply with the order and that there was no way of knowing whether the central government would have assisted it. On this basis, it could be argued that this is a fairly narrow authority, which depended on the fact that the dependant was a poor local authority that would take twenty-two years to bring its entire road network into a satisfactory condition. But on the other hand, the Court showed sensitivity to the general financial implications of colossal expenditure for public bodies for it offered, as a supporting argument, the notion that (at 88) 'the

Oireachtas is not a party to these proceedings and, presumably, having regard to the separation of powers could not be'. This somewhat gnomic observation could be seen as an acknowledgement of the independence of the legislature from the Courts and, in particular, of the rather basic idea that it is for the Dáil to vote supply. The notion of 'supply' means that large-scale public expenditure is to be decided by the Dáil. This factor is the reason why public expenditure always has to be authorized in the annual Estimates and Appropriation Act, despite the fact that there is also always in existence an earlier statutory duty to provide the service that requires the expenditure. This duality has great significance because it means that even the Government is not competent to spend public funds unless these have been voted in the annual Estimates. This bar is based on the idea that items of public expenditure must be decided annually by the Dáil , on the advice of the elected Government, at a time when each item can be seen in the perspective of tax income and of total Government expenditure. The significance of this when it comes to assessing the appropriateness of a court's taking decisions in this area is that, of course, a court is never in a position to make such a comparison.

The third set of authorities are a group grounded on the Article 42.4 guarantee of 'free primary education'. In a typical example of these, *DB*,[2] Kelly J. granted mandatory injunctions compelling the Minister for Health to provide suitable secure facilities and services for the treatment of disturbed children. These facilities and services would necessitate public expenditure of several million pounds. One way in which these authorities could be distinguished from *Brady* is on the basis that they were held to concern education, which is dealt with explicitly in the Constitution. Furthermore, the Department of Health had already drawn up a draft scheme for the treatment of disturbed children, on which the court could draw for guidance. A third point of distinction is that the decision protected the interests of a minority neglected by the political mainstream. In the light of these three differences, it may be just about possible to reconcile *DB* with *Brady* and to confine it fairly narrowly to its own unusual facts.

More recently, the Supreme Court to some extent qualified this line of authority in *Sinnott v Minister for Education, The Irish Times* 13 July 2001, a test case taken on behalf of an autistic man. Here too, the result rested squarely on the meaning to be given to the expression 'free primary education' in Article 42.4. By a six to one majority, the Court overturned the High Court's order that it meant that the State should provide free education for the applicant, appropriate to his needs, for as long as he could benefit from it. But it is significant that the Supreme Court did rule that his constitutional rights gave him an entitlement to appropriate education up to the age of 18.

Concluding Comment

The following observations are sufficiently broad to apply to both the taxation and public expenditure cases. In the first place, it might be thought that on a reading of the express terms of the Constitution, a good case could be made for the view that taxation and public expenditure should be treated by the courts in the same way as any other subjects. This would follow from the notion of the Rule of Law – that is, that the executive-legislature (an expression intended to capture the fact that the executive, through its party majority, controls the legislature) is subject to the Constitution just as much as is any private citizen. Or, to put it another way, individual rights important enough to be recognized by the Constitution must be enforceable, and the High and Supreme Courts are the bodies with the duty and authority to do this. As it was put by Kelly J. in *DB*, 'the Minister for Health is not immune from a court order vindicating the personal rights of a citizen.'

However, as against this, it is suggested that a more sophisticated understanding of our constitutional–political system dictates great caution. This view may be justified and articulated in a number of ways. One of these is the historical origin of the 1937 Constitution and, in particular, the deliberate crafting of

Article 45, entitled 'Directive Principles of Social Policy', which establishes a number of socio-economic guarantees but then goes on to state explicitly that they 'shall be in the care of the Oireachtas exclusively and shall not be cognisable by Court'. The history of the Constitution's drafting has been summarized thus:

> De Valera's drafting team agreed it was clear that many of these socioeconomic fundamental rights guarantees [which were included in early drafts] could be invoked as to create very difficult situations. The drafting team then moved many of them into an entirely new clause, Article 45, which they headed Directive Principles of Social Policy. . . . The exception was the free primary education provisions of Article 42.4, the only enforceable socioeconomic right in the Constitution.[3]

The second feature which bears on the question is the Separation of Powers and the superior legitimacy which this establishes for the political organs, in the taxation–public expenditure field. (This is something which was alluded to in both the *Cavan* pot-holes case and *Sinnott*). The significant point here is the incapacity of a court to take into account all the factors which are relevant. An example of this is the *DB* case. It was a strong point in the plaintiff's favour that on the particular facts of the case, the policy of how to provide the units required by the plaintiff had already been worked out though not implemented by the Department, so that the court was not obliged to do this itself. (However, unfortunately, Kelly J. indicated that he would have been prepared to make the order, even had this feature been absent.) In addition, in *Murphy,* we have pointed out factors (compensating advantages of married status) which a court is not competent to take into account. This militates in favour of a court avoiding this territory.

In short, I believe that in *Murphy* and, to a lesser extent in *D.B.*, the courts did not observe the dangers and difficulties of their involvement in these areas as fully as they might. It seems inappropriate for an unelected body to assert the power both to reduce taxes and to increase public expenditure.

7. Procedure and Process

This chapter focuses not upon the substance of what is being done but upon the process and procedure through which it is accomplished, in several disparate areas: pre-trial criminal procedure; access to the courts themselves; public administration; and elections and referenda. Procedure in such significant fields has correctly been regarded as important in that it draws with it such important values as accessibility to information; impartiality; accountability and openness. As well as being important in themselves, these considerations will often have an impact on the quality of the substantive decision that eventually emerges. We shall see these generalizations illustrated as we turn to consider the judges' work in using the Constitution to effect change in these areas.

I Criminal Procedure

The major headline for the Courts' decisions in this area is Article 38.1 which states that: 'no person shall be tried on any criminal charge save in due course of law'. These pregnant words have launched if not a thousand, then a dozen improvements to statute law. For instance: the right to a speedy trial, based on the idea that justice delayed is justice denied (*The State (O'Connell) v Fawsitt* [1986] IR 362); the right to legal representation (*The State (Healy) v Donoghue* [1976] IR 325); right to advice from a solicitor, when the accused is in custody (*Heaney v Ireland* [1994] 3 IR 593); the rule that unconstitutionally (though not illegally) obtained evidence must normally be excluded (see Casey, pp. 423–28); the precept that a criminal offence should be precisely defined which meant that the offence of 'loitering with intent' under the Vagrancy Act 1824 was struck down (*King v Att. Gen.* [1981] IR 233); and the requirement that there must be some proportionality between the gravity of an offence and the punishment prescribed for it (*Cox v Ireland* [1992] 2 IR 503). A further example concerns the principle, contained in Article 38, that no person may be tried on any criminal charge without a jury. It has been held that the Juries Act 1927 (which excluded from jury service both citizens who did not pay rates above a specified figure and women, unless they made positive application to sit as a juror) was unconstitutional in that it failed to fulfil the requirement that the jury should be a representative cross-section of the community (*de Burca v Att. Gen.* [1976] IR 38).

More controversial was the steady holding by the Supreme Court (in *The People (Attorney General) v O'Callaghan* [1966] IR 501 and *Ryan v DPP* [1989] IR 399 that bail cannot be refused on the ground that it is expected that the accused might commit another offence while out on bail. This view, which had made Ireland the most liberal state in Western Europe on this point, was reversed by constitutional amendment in 1996 (passed, as it happens, by a majority of about three to one).

However, where it is appropriate, the judges have been flexible and prepared to recognize that changed circumstances may require a qualification of traditional rights. For instance, it has been held that the verdict of a jury need not be unanimous but (as is provided by the Criminal Justice Act 1984) may be satisfied by a majority of ten to two (*O'Callaghan v Att. Gen.* [1993] 2 IR 17). Again, in *O'Leary v A.G.* [1993] I IR 102, (105) it was said that a section creating a rebuttable presumption that a person found in possession of incriminating documents is a member of an illegal organization was not unconstitutional, despite the fact that this reversed the normal onus of proof. And *Heaney v Ireland* [1994] 3 IR 593 held that in certain circumstances the right to silence could be abridged by the creation of an offence of failing to account for one's movements.[1]

The Constitution permits an exemption from the general right to jury trial in the case of 'minor offences' (Article 38.2) and in defining this significant phrase, the Courts have been less convincing. In the first place, they have reached the unexceptionable conclusion that the main factor is the severity of the sentence. But the particular difficulty here arises where the punishment goes beyond imprisonment or a fine and includes (say) a disqualification from driving or the confiscation of the contraband in a conviction for smuggling. The Courts have stigmatized such elements of the possible punishments as secondary, and have declined to take them into account in measuring the severity of an offence in deciding whether there is a right to jury trial. Given that, for example, the loss of a wine licence, which was treated as merely 'secondary' in *The State (Pheasantry Ltd) v Donnelly* [1982] ILRM 512, had the effect of reducing the value of the premises from £40,000 to £7,500, there is an air of illogicality and unreality about this distinction which Kelly, Hogan and Whyte have characterized as 'one of the less convincing exercises of the Supreme Court since the era of judicial activism began' (p. 633).

II Right of Access to a Court

The policy that the courts have, on the whole, followed here is set out in the following words of O'Higgins C.J. in *Condon v Minister for Labour* [1981] IR 62, 69:

> A strong, healthy and concerned public opinion may, in the words of Edmund Burke, 'snuff the approach of tyranny in every tainted breeze', but effective resistance to unwarranted encroachment of constitutional guarantees and rights, depends, in the ultimate analysis, on the courts. If access to the courts is denied or prevented or obstructed, then such encroachment, being unchallenged, may become habitual, and, therefore, unacceptable.

We may consider this question first in relation to rights under private law (contract, tort, property, etc.); and, secondly, as regards the control of public authorities by public law. Not surprisingly, perhaps, the answer is broadly the same in each area, namely that, in the more extreme cases, the judges have been active in invoking the Constitution to remove obstructions to bringing one's case before the courts.

Private Law

First, in the field of private law, the 'right to litigate a justiciable controversy' (i.e. a controversy which may be resolved by law) has been a significant vehicle for change. In *Macauley v Minister for Posts* [1966] IR 345 it was discerned as one of the 'unenumerated personal rights' which could be quarried from Article 40.3.1. Before Mrs Macauley could sue the Minister for an allegedly inadequate phone service, she had to reckon with a statutory provision stating that a plaintiff could sue a Minister only after the permission of the Attorney General had been obtained – and this despite the fact that the Attorney General was a colleague of the Minister. Kennedy J. struck down this provision, which was anachronistic and traceable back to the position of the King of England in the Middle Ages. A not dissimilar rule of common law – that the State is immune from action in tort – met its end in *Byrne v Ireland* [1972] IR 241, which was an action brought by a plaintiff who had fallen into an inadequately lit trench dug by the Minister for Posts (or, as seems much more likely, dug on behalf of the Minister!). Had the trench been dug by a private person, for instance a builder, this would probably have been an 'open and shut' case. As it was, the plaintiff could commence the case proper only after the Supreme Court had established that, whatever statute or common law may say, there is a constitutional 'right to litigate a justiciable controversy'.

These cases involved rather exotic relics. Another line of authority concerns the Statute of Limitations 1957 which lays down a period of limitations within which a plaintiff must commence proceedings or be forever barred. Obviously, the sensible policy underlying such provisions is to prevent stale claims menacing defendants long after all the evidence has been forgotten. However, in exceptional cases this may amount to an unfair restriction on the right of access to a court. An example, identified in *O'Brien v Keogh* [1972] IR 144 is where a parent of a child happened to be both the plaintiff (on behalf of the child) and also defendant because it was the parent's behaviour (for example, negligent driving) which had caused the harm. But *O'Brien* was questioned in *Moynihan v Greensmyth* [1977] IR 55 on the basis that if there had been an inexcusable and inordinate delay, the claim ought to be struck out, this time out of justice to the defendant. It was rather poor judge-craft of the court not to mention this in *O'Brien*.

In the most recent authority, *Tuohy v Courtney* [1994] 3 IRI, 47, in declining to strike down a limitation period, the Supreme Court struck a fairly non-interventionist note. Finlay C.J. stated (at 47):

> What has to be balanced is the constitutional right of the plaintiff to litigate against two other contesting rights or duties, firstly, the constitutional right of the defendant in his property to be protected against unjust or burdensome claims and, secondly, the public interest which is involved in the avoidance of state claims. In such a balancing function, the role of the courts is not to impose their view of the correct or desirable balance in substitution for the view of the legislature but rather to determine from an objective stance whether the balance contained in the impugned legislation is so contrary to reason and fairness as to constitute an unjust attack on some individual's constitutional rights.

Public Law

Locus standi is an important preliminary requirement by which a person can only bring proceedings in respect of the constitutionality of a law or the legality of an administrative action if the law or administrative action has caused him some injury or loss, which has not been suffered by other members of the community. This rule was the product of the historic common law notion that there should be no special compartment of law or system of courts for the State. In consequence, public law developed as a department of private law, with the same requirement that the person taking action should have actually suffered loss.

There was also a rather unlikely fear of the litigant who litigates for a laugh. In any case, the rule meant that where some public body committed an unlawful act which harmed the community but made no direct impact on a person's rights, then – classically – there was a danger that no one would be regarded as competent to take action.

The relevance of this rule to the present chapter is that if it had been stringently applied it would have had the effect of reducing the courts' involvement in the major constitutional scene so that infringements of the Constitution would have gone unchecked. In fact, however, the Irish courts have – in effect – substantially watered down the *locus standi* requirement. We need not go into the various judicial formulations and re-formulations – the significant point is that in several high-profile cases[2] want of *locus standi* has not been allowed to be an obstacle in the path of a litigant with a serious point about some governmental action which was allegedly unlawful or unconstitutional.

Given the importance of government under the law and the belated recognition that public law is different from private law, the effective removal of *locus standi* was plainly correct and realistic.

But there are two recent cases in which the policy of maintaining open access to the courts, especially in the case of unpopulated minorities, was not, or at any rate, not fully, followed. First, in *Croke v Smith (No. 2)* [1998] 1 IR 101, the Supreme Court considered a provision of the Mental Treatment Act 1945 by which a person could be detained in a mental hospital, provided only that two medical practitioners had certified that the patient was of unsound mind. Thus, although here the right to liberty, traditionally the highest of all constitutional values, was at stake, the court rejected the argument that an automatic, independent review of the justification for detention was required. Instead, it held that the availability of judicial review sufficed, despite the fact that in judicial review the scope of the High Court's jurisdiction to intervene is rather circumscribed (an argument which had been accepted by the European

Court of Human Rights in a case involving the British equivalent of the arrangements under review in *Croke*. See *X v U.K.* [1981] 4 EHRR 181). Another case in which the policy of keeping open access to courts might appear not to have been followed is *Re Article 26 and the Illegal Immigrants (Trafficking) Bill 1999* [2000] 2 IR 360. The central issue in this reference was whether Article 34.3.1° (establishing access to the High Court) was violated by a provision which restricted a failed asylum-seeker to 14 days – yes, 14 days – within which to seek judicial review. The Supreme Court upheld the Bill; but – it is significant – only on the basis of an exceptional provision in the Bill, which allowed the High Court a discretion to extend the 14-day period so as to allow sufficient access to the courts to satisfy the applicant's constitutional right in the circumstances of the case.

III Controlling Public Administration by way of Judicial Review

This field of law is only tangentially connected to the (written) Constitution. However, devising this law is a central part of the judge's task of keeping the administrative state under the control of law. So some very brief comments on judicial review of administrative action are included here. This field of law takes two forms: fair procedure, and substantive control (sometimes known as 'reasonableness').

Fair procedure looms very large in the control of the actions of public bodies in all common law jurisdictions, especially Ireland, where it has been re-christened 'constitutional justice'. The notion that a fair procedure lays the ground for a good substantive outcome has been taken to heart. Professor Wade has remarked: 'the whole theory of "natural justice" is that Ministers, though free to decide as they like, will, in practice, decide properly and responsibly once the facts have been laid fairly before them' (1949) 10 Cam L.J. 217.

The result has been that over the past two or three decades dozens of cases have built up a framework of constitutional justice, within which public administrators must keep. The main channel (we are not dealing here with the 'no bias' rule) of consti-tutional justice means, in the first place, that before an administrator takes a decision against an individual (in the fields of, say, award of a grant; removal from employment; compulsory acquisition of land, or the grant of a licence), the individual must be alerted to the case against him. Specifically he must be notified of the following:

(i)   that a decision adverse to the person affected is in contem-plation;

(ii)   the grounds upon which the action is to be taken;

(iii)   all information relevant to the issue, including details of the case against and (probably) in favour of the person affected; and

(iv)   the possible consequences of the decision – sanctions, etc.

In addition, the individual affected by the (anticipated) decision must be allowed the opportunity and facilities to make the best case possible against the decision. On the whole, this has been a constructive and (given its wide ramifications) significant devel-opment. Indeed, in many areas, the legislature has followed the trial blazed by the judiciary. An example is the duty to give reasons first established by case-law in the late 1980s and 1990s, but now confirmed and widened by the Freedom of Infor-mation Act 1997 s.18.

But there ought to be a balance between individual proce-dural rights and the interest of the community in government administration being allowed to proceed smoothly to the benefit of the great majority, without administrators (who are not knowledgeable in the sometimes artificial and unexpected devices of the law) being distracted by legal elephant traps. Let me take two examples where I think that the judiciary may have gone too far. One of the patriarchal cases in this area of the law is *Kiely v Minister for Social Welfare (No. 2)* [1977] IR 267 which arose after the appellant's husband had suffered an accident at work which caused severe burns and led eventually to depres-sion. A few months later he died and the appellant, K, claimed a death benefit under the Social Welfare (Occupational Injuries) Act 1966. Her claim was heard by the deciding officer and, on appeal, the appeals officer in the Department of Social Welfare. The particular feature of *Kiely* which is relevant here concerned the behaviour of the medical assessor who had sat with the appeals officer and, in a way which seemed natural to him, had asked questions (of a medical nature) of the applicant's expert medical witness. Henchy J. stated:

> It ill becomes an assessor who is an affiliate of the quasi-judicial officer, to descend into the forensic arena . . . the taint of partiality will necessarily follow if [the appeals officer or assessor] intervenes to such an extent as to appear to be presenting or conducting the case against the claimant.

Here, despite the conventional rubric quoted earlier in the judgment about tribunals being allowed to follow a less formal procedure than that expected of a court, the court seems to have imposed upon the appeals officer (a medium-level civil servant) and his medical assessor the sort of procedure which a court follows. Yet this will often be inappropriate and artificial in a forum in which most applicants represent themselves, so that their cases will often benefit from pointed, though not hostile, questioning.

By way of introduction to the next case, *Gallagher v Corrigan* (unreported High Court, 1 February 1988) let us notice the common situation in which in the nature of things, the person affected must have a pretty fair idea of the case against him, although he has not been explicitly informed about it by the public body. In other cases, the law has accommodated this feature of common experience by the notion that if the plaintiff 'well knew'[3] of the particular aspect of the case against him, he cannot claim that he should have had explicit notice. By contrast, *Gallagher* set a rather high standard of explicitness and formality in regard to the warning which the public authority must give to the person affected. The case arose out of the purported disciplining of four prison officers – the applicants in the case – following on the escape of a prisoner from St. Patrick's Institution. Blayney J. posed the following question:

> Was the ['hear the other side' rule] complied with ? . . . It was submitted . . . that the reports of Chief Officer O'Sullivan, which were furnished to the applicants, endorsed by the Deputy Governor 'for explanation please' constituted charges of negligence. In my opinion they did not. They were addressed to the Deputy Governor. *The only part that was addressed to the applicants was the endorsement of the Deputy Governor 'for explanation please.'* The purpose was clearly to obtain from each of the applicants, and from the other six officers who were also asked for an explanation, information which when pieced together would enable the Deputy Governor to come to a conclusion as to how the escape occurred. . . . The applicants may have had reason to believe that if they did not give a satisfactory explanation of how they had performed their duties on the day of the escape, they might be charged with negligence, but they had no reason to believe that *such a charge had been preferred against them.*[4] (My emphasis).

In summary, in each of these cases, the courts appear to have applied their own procedure – the accusatorial procedure, accompanied by elaborate formality – to institutions of public administration. There has sometimes been a failure to advert to the fact that such institutions are subtly different and should be treated differently.

Another feature of the law in the field of constitutional justice which may be queried is the steady holding that, if a decision is taken in breach of these rules, the defect is not cured by the provision of a right of appeal at which stage the rules are fully observed. Take, for instance, *Moran v A.G.* [1976] IR 400 in which a taxi-driver licence was withdrawn by a Garda Superintendent (because the taxi driver had been found guilty of larceny). The Superintendent did not allow the taxi driver to put his side of the case. The issue of whether or not he would have had anything to say, if he had been allowed the opportunity, was not regarded as affecting the matter: fair procedure is taken to be 'a good' of itself, irrespective of its immediate practical result. Nor was it regarded as relevant that the driver could, under the statute, have appealed against the removal of his licence to the District Court, where he would have had a full hearing but chose not to do so.

We have dwelt much on procedural rights because these are of especial importance in the field of public administration. Substantive rights are somewhat less significant because considerable latitude has to be allowed to administrators acting under the direction of elected politicians. However, even in the substantive field, courts have called ministers, local authorities or other administrators to account if they have gone beyond certain limits, while at the same time respecting the principle that if the legislature vests a decision in an administrator rather than a court, it is because it wishes to draw on the wisdom and experiences of the administrator.

An early instance is *Listowel v McDonagh* [1968] IR 312, 318. Here the relevant statutory provision authorized a local authority 'to prohibit the erection of temporary dwellings if the authority was of the opinion that such erection would be prejudicial to public health.' Purporting to act under this power, Listowel UDC made an order banning the construction of temporary dwellings on a number of named streets. The defendant was convicted of the offence and fined ten shillings. His principal line of defence was that the by-law had been made in bad faith in that the local authority was really trying to rid Listowel of itinerants. The Supreme Court agreed with this line of defence.

Sometimes the common law heads of review are augmented by the idea that the administrator must respect values protected by the Constitution. An example is *Fajujonu v Minister for Justice* [1990] ILRM 234, the facts of which were that the first two applicants were aliens, a husband and wife, who had come to reside in Ireland. The family had lived illegally within the State for some years and the third applicant was their daughter who had been born in Ireland and was, therefore, an Irish citizen. In these proceedings, they sought an order that the parents should not be deported. Deportation would have meant that the daughter would be faced with the dilemma of either being compulsorily separated from her parents, in breach of her constitutional family rights, or alternatively, being forced to leave the State of which she was a citizen, again a breach of her constitutional rights. It was significant that although the parents were illegal immigrants, they had otherwise done nothing wrong. The resolution of the matter reached by the Supreme Court was that the Minister should only deport the first applicant if he were 'satisfied that for good and sufficient reason the "common good" required it.' (at 239). This is conventionally regarded as a very high hurdle to jump and one which makes Irish law in this area more liberal than the standard imposed by the European Convention on Human Rights.

IV Elections and Referenda

The field of electoral law and procedure (of which one example, *,McKenna v Ireland* No. 2, is given at pp. 4–5) has a legitimate claim to be regarded as the one in which the judges have made most impact on the political system, indeed on its very centre of gravity. Moreover, the 'mother of them all' of this line of authority – *O'Donovan v A.G.* [1961] IR 114 – came very early in the era of judicial activism. The background to this case was that successive governments had found that the opportunity to gerrymander the electoral system as presented by their control of the Oireachtas, which makes Electoral Acts, constituted a temptation that was more than political flesh and blood could bear. In *O'Donovan,* the then Fianna Fáil Government had allocated more seats per head of population to the rural areas, where their party was strongest. Striking down the law in the High Court, Budd J. fastened upon Article 16.2.3, which states that 'the ratio between the number of members . . . for each constituency and the population . . . should, so far as it is practicable, be the same throughout the country'. It was held that the dominant principle of this provision was 'one man – one vote – one value', qualified only 'by the lesser considerations of practicability' in holding the election. In particular, Budd J. rejected the main thrust of the Government's defence. This was that factors like the greater expenditure of time in servicing the constituencies and 'going about persecuting civil servants' (in Professor Chubb's well-known phrase) in sparse rural constituencies justified such a discrepancy as that of 30% between South Galway and Dublin (South West).[5]

Again, in *McMahon v A.G.* [1972] IR 69, the Supreme Court drew upon the reference to a 'secret ballot' (in Article 16.1.4) to rule that the statutory regulations, which authorized the same number being printed on both the counterfoil and on the back of the ballot, was unconstitutional. The reason was that matching the two might enable someone who had surreptitiously gained access to the ballot materials to discover how an elector had voted. This seemed a rather far-fetched argument. However, Ó Dálaigh C.J. met the contention that, in the real world, the chances of this happening were slim by an interesting remark: 'Constitutional rights are declared not alone because of the bitter memoirs of the past but not less because of the improbable, but not-to-be-overlooked perils of the future'.

8. The Separation of Powers

I General Operation of the Doctrine

In the next field to procedure and process is the design and inter-relationship of governmental institutions and here too the judges have taken an active line in seeking to make improve-ments. The main vehicle that they have adopted is the Separation of Powers,[1] a broad doctrine that has been floating around in political thought for several centuries and is to be found, in some version or other, in the constitutions of many states. In a general form, the doctrine has been explained as follows: 'There are three main classes of governmental functions: the legislative, the executive and the judicial, and for each, there should be a matching organ of government, with the organs being independent of each other.'[2]

In a modified form, the Separation of Powers is a central feature of the Constitution. It is dealt with mainly – as might be expected – in three provisions, one each for the legislature, executive and judiciary. First: no law is to be made save by the Oireachtas (Article 15.2.1°); secondly, the 'executive power of the State' (in both domestic and foreign affairs) is vested in the Government (Articles 28.2 and 29.4.1°). Finally, only the courts may exercise the judicial function save in the case of 'limited functions' in the non-criminal field (Articles 34.1 and 37.1).

However, our concern here is not the statement of the Separation of Powers to be found in the Constitution but rather with the use made of it by Irish judges. In fact, as regards the judicial function and organ, Irish judges have given the doctrine a more stringent application than it has received in other jurisdictions (notably the U.S. or Australia) where the doctrine also occupies a central constitutional position.

II The Judicial Function

The main feature of the Separation of Powers is that there should be no illegitimate interference with a court and, secondly, that all judicial functions (a.k.a. 'the administration of justice') must be vested in a court. Taking first the non-interference limb, we find a number of sensible decisions which can be illustrated by the early case of *Buckley v A.G.* [1950] IR 67 which involved a striking infringement upon the judicial process, by way of an *ad hominem* act of the Oireachtas which specifically settled the results of a pending court case. A less spectacular example occurred in *Maher v A.G.* [1973] IR 140 in which the Supreme Court considered a section which provided that a certificate, stating that a specimen of a person's blood contained a specific concentration of alcohol, was to be taken as '*conclusive* evidence' of that fact (my italics). The section was held unconstitutional because the Constitution reserves to the courts 'the determination of all the essential ingredients of any offence charged against an accused person.' Had the court not reached this conclusion, the result would have been that a doctor could not have been cross-examined as to whether there had been any possibility of error in his analysis of the blood sample. A second example is *Brennan v Minister for Justice* [1995] 1 IR 612, outlined above at p. 5).

But in some cases, the courts' zeal in this area has, it is suggested, gone too far, for principle or practicality. Three examples have already been mentioned.[3] Let us take three others, which each concern the precept that all instances of 'the judicial function' must be vested in a court. In the first place, this provision has been interpreted to mean that the functions of disciplining professionals such as lawyers or doctors for (non-trivial) misconduct cannot be dealt with unaided by the relevant professional body, for example the Law Society. Instead, they must also involve the High Court, not merely on appeal, but in the re-hearing of all the evidence, which has already been heard once before the professional body: *Re Solicitors* [1960] IR 239.

Now, on the technical–legal plane, the definition of 'the judicial function' is very problematic and the Supreme Court's finding that disciplining solicitors amounted to an exercise of the judicial function was anything but compelling. Accordingly, it seems reasonable to conclude that *Re Solicitors* and the cases that followed it were grounded on a policy view, namely that, bearing in mind how much is often at stake – a professional career – it was only the Court which could be trusted as entirely impartial. But this view is flawed on two grounds. First of all, the present arrangement means that before an erring professional person can be disciplined, two fairly high hurdles must be jumped. A finding of professional misconduct must be secured initially before the professional's peers, which will usually not be easy; and then the process has, in effect, to be repeated before the High Court, which makes for further expense, delay and possibly embarrassment of the witnesses, who will usually be patients/clients of the practitioner. In short, the process of discipline is made very cumbersome. Especially in a marginal case, this creates some pressure against disciplinary proceedings. The result of this invocation of the Separation of Powers by the judiciary is that great store is set by protecting the interest of the individual, at substantial cost to the community interest of having competent, ethical practitioners. As we have seen, a similar policy choice has also been made by the judges in several other contexts.

There is another and rather straightforward point. If a professional disciplinary tribunal is prejudiced in any direction, in most cases it will be in favour of, rather than against, the professional before it. Whatever about 'dog doesn't eat dog', it is certainly the case that doctor doesn't eat doctor. In the exceptional case in which the reverse is true – for instance, if the person brought before the disciplinary tribunal is unpopular within his profession because (say) he has been publicly criticizing some of his colleagues – then another and more flexible rule is available to ensure that justice is done. This is simply to put the case, openly and directly, on the basis of the need for impartiality – in other words, the first limb of the well-established rules of fair procedure known as 'constitutional justice' – rather than invoking the present cumbersome arrangement with the High Court being involved in every instance of professional misconduct. If this were done it would mean greater flexibility, in that there would be a range of possibilities, rather than the involvement of a court in every case. (There are other alternative forms of supervision over the disciplinary process: Article 34.3.1° makes it subject to the High Court judicial review jurisdiction and Article 6.1 of the European Convention of Human Rights requires the process to be vested in 'an independent and impartial tribunal' and not necessarily a court of law).

There are now some slight signs (*Keady v Commissioner of Garda Síochána* [1992] 2 IR 197, on the system for disciplining gardaí) that *Re Solicitors* is no longer as popular with some of the judges as formerly. However, the fact remains that the entire structure for professional discipline in the medical, dental, nursing and veterinary professions – as well, of course, as solicitors – has been shaped, I would say distorted, by *Re Solicitors*.

The second example concerns the extremely important area of compensation for personal injuries. It would mean a great improvement in terms of legal costs and delay for the parties and the saving of court time if such cases could be brought before an independent compensation tribunal. However, it seems probable that, because of the Separation of Powers, this task could not be transferred to a tribunal, at any rate without the consent of both parties or some other substantial restriction on its usefulness.[4]

Take, finally, cases dealing with post-trial functions, in the criminal field. As to sentencing, it has been held that this is an aspect of the judicial function and consequently has to be determined by a court (*Deaton v A.G.* [1963] IR 171). Consider, from the same field, the special verdict of 'guilty but insane' (under the Trial of Lunatics Act 1883). This verdict establishes that the accused has performed the murder but that he was not sane at the time of the deed. Accordingly, he is imprisoned until it is safe to release him. The issue here is the simple question of who decides when it is safe to release the prisoner: is it the court of trial or the Minister for Justice? The Supreme Court (in *D.P.P. v Gallagher* [1991] ILRM 339, 344-45) ruled that the correct answer was the court, on the basis that the operation of the 1883 Act did not impact upon the judicial function and so is not a matter for a court. Rather 'it is part of the carrying out of the Executive's role in caring for society and the protection of the common good'. This includes the detention of the accused until the Executive is satisfied that, having regard to the accused's current mental health (and not the character of the offence), it is safe to release him.

The significant point here is that because of the importance assigned by the Irish courts to the Separation of Powers, the debate was cast in terms of characterizing a function as either executive or judicial. Contrast the approach taken by the European Court of Human Rights, in *T v The United Kingdom*

16.12.1999 ECHR (a.k.a. the Jeremy Bulger case) which centred upon the fact that, in Britain, the power to set the minimum term of an indefinite prison sentence is vested in the Home Secretary. The Court held that this was contrary to Article 6.1 of the European Convention in that parole decisions should be taken by independent and impartial bodies.

Yet, in Irish law, because of the dogmatic application of the Separation of Powers, it would seem (from *Deaton*) to be unconstitutional to vest sentencing in a tribunal consisting of well-qualified and independent people like lawyers or doctors, simply because this would not be a court. By contrast, it appears from *Gallagher* that it would be constitutional to vest the parole function, determining how much of a sentence a person need serve based on his conduct in prison, in the Minster for Justice, on the basis that this function could be classified as executive rather than judicial. How much wiser it would be to hold that each function – sentencing and parole – involved the most precious value of liberty. Consequently both should be determined not by a Minister but by an independent body. However, such a body need not necessarily be a court but could be an independent tribunal. This was effectively the position reached by the European Court, but not here, because of the corset of the Separation of Powers.

III Judges Involved in Extra-Curial Activities

One aspect of the separation of the judicial power, which has been almost totally neglected, concerns the fact that the judges have taken on so many extra-curial duties. The most prominent of these is acting as the chairperson of a Tribunal of Inquiry (something which is not required by the Constitution or any other law; but is only a matter of firm convention). In addition, judges have acted as chairpersons of the Dáil Éireann Constituency Commission, the Ethics Commission, the Forum on (Northern Ireland) Peace and Reconciliation, the Second Commission on the Status of Women, the Law Reform Commission, and commissions of inquiry into, for instance, criminal procedure or the Garda.[5]

The advantage of using judges in such roles lies in the fact that the judges are (rightly) trusted by Everyman and Everywoman. Their involvement thus engenders public confidence in the work of (say) the Ethics Commission. But there is plainly a danger in such use. It is that if the judiciary becomes involved in so many broadly political areas it may cease to be regarded as entirely politically neutral. This danger may take three forms. In the first place, a case may present itself before a judge in court concerning some matter with which the judge had dealt earlier, when wearing a different hat. A straightforward example of this arose out of a High Court Judge's role as Chairperson of the Second Commission for the Status of Women. As Chairperson (with the other members of the Commission), she had sent a letter to the Government making the argument that the protocol to the Maastricht Treaty, negotiated by the Government, was too limited as regards abortion, in that it did not permit even counselling within Ireland. Later, she happened to be the judge who was sitting on two abortion information cases in 1992 and 1994, respectively. In such a situation it is desirable and possible for the judge to withdraw. This the judge did in the first case in 1992 but declined to do in another case in 1994 (*Dublin Well Women v Ireland* [1995] ILRM408, 421). On this occasion, one of the parties to the case – SPUC – appealed successfully to the Supreme Court for an order directing her not to hear the case. The Court made it clear that it granted the order not on the ground of actual bias, but on the basis that bias might have been suspected by the appellant.

Secondly, even if Judge A who had an earlier involvement with a case through some tribunal or commission, does not sit on the case, Judge B will have to do so. In this case, a difficulty arises from the fact that, in the public mind, the judiciary is perceived as having a common identity – they are all members of a small high caste, carefully depersonalized by their wigs and gowns. The public may well feel that if one judge is involved in some commission with a broadly political mission, his or her cloak of partial political involvement is thrown over the court system as a whole. The third danger is that the connection between the judicial and broadly political fields may have an effect in the reverse direction. For there is a risk that it might be suspected by some member of the public (however ridiculous the suspicion in reality) that a judge sitting on a tribunal or commission may be influenced in this work by the hope of promotion to a higher court.

In sum, if a close connection between the judges and the political–policy area means that the impartiality and trustworthiness associated with the former will rub off on the latter, then, in the long term, the reverse process is also possible. Strangely – such is the confidence in the judiciary, not least among the judiciary – this point has seldom been noticed. In *Haughey v Moriarty* [1999] 33 IR 52 one of the scattergun of arguments raised by the plaintiff was that it was contrary to Article 34.3 of the Constitution for a judge to chair a Tribunal of Inquiry and the argument received very short shrift.

One exception to the lack of interest in this area is the Constitutional Review Group of 1996, which did take the issue seriously. It stated (at p. 183):

> This may be undesirable as such judges risk becoming publicly identified with the policies of the group or body concerned or may be put in a position of either critic or supporter of the Government. It is important for public confidence in the judiciary and public perception of their independence and impartiality that judges do not directly or indirectly make public statements on matters of policy.

Another distinguished voice urging caution in the presentation is Keane J. who has described the present issue as 'one of no little difficulty' (*Application of Neilan* [1990] 2IR267, 278). It is not as if judges have to be used for the sort of tasks under discussion. Greater use could be made of retired judges or civil servants, academics, or the nominees of professional bodies, like the Law Society.

IV Concluding Comment

The most important point illustrated by the overview of five areas, in this and the preceding chapter, is that the courts have taken the design, process and procedures of the institutions that make decisions at least as seriously as they have taken substantive rules. This should occasion no surprise. Rather obviously, procedure has a direct effect on the substantive outcome. This is obviously true of, for example, the electoral field, and we have referred to the same phenomenon in the field of public administration.

In the cases of criminal procedure – because serious consequences for an unpopular minority are involved – the judges have traditionally been alert to protect the rights of this minority. And in the field of access to courts the importance of good process and convenient access is self-evident: for the court is the forum where the citizens meet their rights, and it is on the feeling that a citizen has had his 'day in Court' that the State's right to say that people should not take the law into their own hands depends.

Again, until the establishment of the Constituency and Referendum Commissions (the latter, at any rate, being a response to the court's work), it was the two political organs exclusively-which ran the electoral system, the very keystone of democracy. Often they did so to the advantage of the majority party. Small wonder, therefore, that the courts should feel it necessary to supervise this area fairly closely.

In most of these areas, the judges, whose particular expertise after all, is procedure, have set sensible balances. However, in the field of the law relating to public administration, it seems that some judges have, in some cases, perhaps with a semi-conscious eye on the court's own elaborate procedure, set too high a standard, leaving traps for lay administrators, to no one's legitimate advantage.

Another patchy area is the Separation of Powers, which was the subject of the present chapter. Here there seems to be a level of misunderstanding of this sprawling, embarnacled doctrine. It seems to have been understood as a vehicle for the judges to make rather far-reaching changes to meet difficulties which could have been met in other less disturbing ways. One example is the notion that certain delicate functions, for instance professional discipline, have to be vested in the often cumbersome procedures of the High Court because they could not be trusted elsewhere. Again, there has been an inadequate understanding that what is sauce for the legislative and executive is also sauce for the judges themselves, and that the Separation of Powers is a divergent doctrine from the Supremacy of the Constitution. What the Supremacy of the Constitution means is that all the organs of the State are subject to the Constitution and, if their activities (be it law or executive action) go beyond the Constitution, then they must be struck down. However, the issue of deciding at what point a law goes beyond the Constitution leaves a great deal of authority to the senior judiciary and one of the major themes of this book is that this authority has been used in a very activist way. In particular, in the present context, it is significant that little attention has been paid to the limit set by the Separation of Powers which states that the elected political organs should have some autonomy from the court's powers of surveillance. To take some examples of formulae of judicial modesty that have not been followed: the judges have been prepared to intervene in the internal proceedings of the Oireachtas;[6] have extended the power of striking down (pre-1937) laws to the District Court and Circuit Court by a very strained interpretation of the Constitution;[7] and have failed to develop a 'political question' doctrine as a judicial no-go area, even in the field of foreign relations.[8]

As a final point, it might be asked why there is so little concern about judges' extra-curial activities and the danger that – in the long term – these might drag the judges into political controversy and reduce their reputation for impartiality, which is their most precious asset. As the House of Lords judge, Lord

Devlin, has remarked extra-judicially, 'The reputation for independence and integrity [of the judges] is a national asset of such richness that one government after another tries to plunder it.'[9]

9. Interpreting the Constitution

I. Overly Literal Interpretation

In the case of an Act of the Oireachtas, the standard watchword for its interpretation is that plain words must be given their plain meaning save where this would lead to an absurdity, whether in the light of common sense or of the policy of the instrument. But the Constitution is different and the judges should not be as concerned with literal interpretation as in the case of an Act. The reason why the Constitution is different is that it was not drafted in the same way, or for the same purpose, as an ordinary statute. In the first place, it covers an unimaginably broader span than any statute: it deals with nothing less than the organs of government and also the relationship between the individual and ordered society. It is addressing a much wider plane than the detailed, concrete provisions of (say) an Occupiers Liability Act. Inevitably, the language and style will be different from the traditional approach to the drafting of a statute, which is thought to justify the operation of certain rather artificial assumptions and rules of formal logic: for example, if a matter is not dealt with explicitly or by very necessary implication, it was not intended; or if something is said twice, it must be intended to mean something fresh and different on the second occasion.

  Several examples of ways in which the Constitution does not conform to the conventional style of legal drafting could be given. Writing extra-judicially Costello J. drew attention to several instances.[1] For example, only the rights to private property and to family are characterized as 'natural rights'. Does this mean that they are to be given a higher level of protection than other fundamental rights, like the right to life? Again, some

Articles provide that the rights they establish may be restricted 'in accordance with law' without providing any limitation whatsoever on the restrictive laws which are thereby authorized. By contrast, the exercise of other rights are made 'subject to public order and morality', whilst another randomly delineated category of rights is made to bow to 'the exigencies of the common good'. Must we attribute different meanings to these three phrases?

Secondly, the Constitution is not only a legal instrument but also an inspirational political document. It is one of the symbols, like the national flag or anthem, through which a polity proclaims to itself and to outsiders: 'This is who we are'. It is a focus of loyalty, a statement of national beliefs, ideals and aspirations. Necessarily, it is written for the citizen–layperson as much as for the lawyer. Indeed, in the U.S. it has been said that the Constitution is 'first of all, a layman's document, not a lawyer's shrivelled contract'. Thirdly, as we now know from the release (in 1987) of the relevant papers, many different persons (often non-lawyers), stages and processes were involved in the drafting of the Constitution. It is hardly surprising that there are some disjunctions and unresolved conflicts between different provisions.

In the light of these points of difference, to interpret the Constitution according to an inflexibly literal rule would be rather like trying to solve a code by using a cipher-key for a different code. Yet the judges have often taken an inappropriately literal approach to interpretation: an approach which would be apt in the case of a statute but not the Constitution. Take first, the judgment of Kelly, Horgan and Whyte, the leading text on the Constitution. Kelly, in passages unusually heart-felt for that austere text, gives some examples of excessively literal decisions (at *xcii*):

> The minute word-by-word interpretation of the Constitution which the last decade has seen bears no relation to the realities of the process by which it was drafted and enacted. The principle of equality of

citizens before the law was a shibboleth long before Article 40.1 put it in a constitutional text. But did anyone in 1937 really intend that the phrase 'as human persons' was to be used to whittle down its significance, rather than as a piece of pious padding? 'Laws' is a word used in the Constitution in several contexts which require it to be understood *in those contexts* as statutes. Does it follow that the continuance provisions of Article 50 do not carry non-statutory law? Or that such a conclusion is warranted by the use of the words 'repealed or amended', when the purpose of drawing such a distinction between these categories of law is not apparent? May we not simply say that the intent of the Article is plain, but its drafting awkward? The Irish text being the authoritative one (however absurd the background of this rule) it is used as an elucidatory aid in construing the English. But does anyone believe that the nameless translators of 1937 (whose work was left virtually without debate in a Dáil most of whose members knew very little Irish anyway) deliberately used the Irish future tense rather than the Irish present (where English grammar would make no distinction) in order to convey that only post-1937 events were contemplated, or that the Government (let alone the Dáil or people) understood the results of such a technique? Such things have however been said or implied by the courts in recent times, and require from the observer an act of good faith of the kind which is normally accorded only to theological propositions (my emphasis).

Later, Kelly surveys the various approaches adopted to constitutional interpretation (literal; broad; harmonious; historical; and natural law) and, in this context, remarks (at p. 5): 'One needs to emphasize, however, that the courts have shown no consistency with regard to any particular approach and this gives rise to the suspicion that individual judges are willing to rely on any such approach as will offer adventitious support for a conclusion which they have already reached.'

A further set of examples comes from the part of the Constitution dealing with the jurisdictions of the various courts. The first line of authority concerns Article 34.4.3, by which '[t]he Supreme Court shall with such exceptions and subject to such regulations as may be presented by law, have appellate jurisdiction from all decisions of the High Court . . . '. In surprising decisions on this provision, it has been held that an appeal lies to the Supreme Court, from the High Court, against the grant of a habeas corpus, a discretionary order as to costs in either civil or criminal matters and committal for civil contempt. Yet, in each of these situations, one would have expected the traditional law – that there is no appeal – to be followed; in the first case (habeas corpus) because of a preference for liberty; and in the other two cases, because the trial court is especially well placed to determine the issue.

A further consequence of Article 34.3.1 is even more surprising. The Supreme Court has applied the provision at its full, literal width to hold that the prosecutor may appeal to the Supreme Court *against* an acquittal in the High Court (Central Criminal Court). In the hotly-contested case of *The People (DPP)* v *O'Shea*, [1982] IR 384 in which this rule was established, the two dissenting judges (Finlay P. and Henchy J.) appealed in vain to the argument that there is, inherently, no appeal from a jury acquittal and to the ancient tradition in the criminal justice system of the rule against double jeopardy.

Another line of interpretation concerns the High Court, the jurisdiction of which extends – according to Article 34.3.1 – to 'all matters and questions whether of law or fact, civil or criminal'. The point that arises here is whether the word 'all' bars the legislature from vesting exclusively a decision in regard to a specified type of case in one of the lower courts. Perhaps surprisingly, an affirmative answer was given by the High Court in *R. v R.* [1984] IR 296. One of the obvious dangers with this finding was that (in the criminal field) an accused might seek to frustrate a prosecution for, say, a parking offence by asserting a right to be tried in the High Court, or that (in the civil field) an economically strong defendant might seek to deter the plaintiff by insisting on having a minor claim tried before the High Court.

However, this lapse into what this author regards as excessive literalism was corrected by the Supreme Court in *Tormey v Attorney General* [1985] IR 289, in which it was held that Article 34.3.1 did not bear its full literal meaning.

To summarize these comments on the cases interpreting the provisions dealing with the jurisdiction of the Supreme Court and the High Court: in the case of appeals to the Supreme Court, literalism reigns; in the case of the High Court, what appears to be common sense eventually prevailed. There seems to be no rationale justifying the divergence of treatment: the cases reviewed in this section all come from the same part of the Constitution. It is notable that in the case of the Supreme Court's jurisdiction, a literal approach has been adopted which has often had the effect of flying in the face of what might be called 'civil liberties' values. Yet in many other cases, as we have seen, civil liberties have been esteemed.[2]

II Purposive Interpretation

There are other areas where there has been a consistent ignoring of literal interpretation. A famous example is *Re Art. 26 and the Emergency Powers Bill 1976* [1977] I.R. 159 in which the Supreme Court appeared to sacrifice the literal interpretation in the interest of a concern for civil liberties. Here the issue concerned Article 28.3.3 (the emergency provision) which states that 'time of war' includes a time when there is taking place an armed conflict in which the State is not a participant but *in respect of which each of the Houses of the Oireachtas shall have resolved* that . . . a national emergency exists [in Ireland]' (my emphasis). But what if there is, despite what the resolutions say, in fact no emergency so that the resolutions are false: can a court 'look behind' them to review their correctness? On a literal reading, the answer must be in the negative. But, in a striking observation, the Supreme Court (at 174) 'expressly reserved [the question] for future consideration'. Here the Court was plainly firing a warning shot across the bows of the executive–legislature, to prevent it from drawing too freely on the open cheque allowed by the words of the Constitution.

Another instance of departure from literal interpretation concerns the courts' extraordinary neglect of the words of Article 8, which attempts to promote the Irish language by declaring it to be 'the national language and the first official language'. Here, there is a very striking contrast between *The State (Cussen) v Brennan* [1981] IR 181 and *Groener v Minister for Education* [1990] ILRM 335. In *Brennan*, the Supreme Court held – despite Article 8 – that the Local Appointments Commissioners had acted *ultra vires* in making a knowledge of Irish one of the qualifications for a medical post in the then Cork Regional Hospital. *Groener* was a European Court of Justice case in which the plaintiff was a Dutch national who had been refused a post as an art lecturer in Dublin because she had failed the Irish test. The facts, in other words, were similar to those in *Brennan;* yet in *Groener,* G's claim failed on the basis that this requirement was in furtherance of a policy for the protection of the constitutionally-protected national language. Surprisingly, *Groener* was decided by the European Court of Justice operating within the framework of European Union law. Nevertheless the European Court allowed itself to be influenced by the respect due to the wording of the Irish Constitution, respect which was conspicuously lacking in *Brennan*. (From *Brennan* and many similar decisions, one can predict very definitely the fate of an action seeking a declaration that all members of the Irish soccer team should have a basic knowledge of the first official language!)

But the most striking example of purposive interpretation of all is the seminal judgment of *Ryan v A.G.* [1965] IR 294. Before the High Court (Kenny J.) decision in *Ryan*, it was generally assumed that the phrase 'personal rights' in Article 40.3.1° simply provided a headline to herald the slightly more specific formulation ('life, person, good name and property rights . . . ') in Article 40.3.2°. Kenny J.'s principle reason for rejecting this conventional wisdom was that the Constitution sets up a 'Christian and democratic state' from which it follows that the citizens of that State should enjoy all the personal rights which are appropriate in such a State. Where these are not mentioned in the Constitution, Article 40.3.1° has been regarded as a reservoir of unspecified rights to make up this deficiency, for example: the right to bodily integrity, the right to free movement (the right to a passport), the right to marry, the right to privacy.

What is significant for present purposes, is that this cascade of fundamental rights gushed from a most purposive feat of interpretation. Put simply, this source of rights exists because the rights were held to be appropriate in the context of the Irish Constitution. But there was nothing in the bare language of the text to suggest this source.

III A Sensible Middle Way

The criticism advanced here may be summarized as follows: first, in several decisions on the interpretation of the Constitution there has been excessive literalism; secondly, courts appear to follow no consistent principle in selecting between a literal and a purposive approach to interpretation. Any criticism of this type has naturally to address the counter-argument: is a better alternative available? In particular, any attack on unqualified literalism leads to the riposte that constitutional interpretation would become merely the unprincipled policy preference of whichever judge happens to hear the case: the very thing that we are seeking to avoid.

Let us consider what answers may be offered to this soft impeachment.

There seem to be two fruitful possibilities. The first guide, which has been used intermittently over a long period, is what has been called 'tradition and consensus'.[3] Two recent examples may be drawn from the field of religious rights. The first of these is *Murphy v Independent Radio and Television Commission* [1997] 2 ILRM 167; [1998] 2 ILRM 360, which centred upon the Radio and Television Act 1988. This Act provides that: 'no advertisement shall be broadcast which is directed towards any religious or political end . . . '. The constitutionality of this provision was squarely raised when the IRTC banned a radio advert which commenced as follows: 'What think ye of Christ? Would you, like Peter, boldly say he is the son of the living God . . . '.

In *Murphy* there was a contest between the right of one religion to spread its message and win converts – in other words to proselytize – and, on the other hand, the preference of another religion not to have its adherents won over to the proselytizing religion. Did not the ban on advertising interfere with the applicant's right to proselytize and, thus, with his right to religious practice? Rejecting this argument, Geoghegan J. in the High Court stated (at 472): 'The prohibition on this advertisement is not an intrusion on *the quiet possession of religious beliefs*' (my emphasis). This sentence seems to be most telling. It indicates that in a case of tension between the right to proselytize and the right to quiet practice, it is the latter which is likely to prevail. In short, flippant terms, freedom of competition does not extend to religion.

The other case is *Campaign to Separate Church and State v Minister for Education* [1998] 2 ILRM 81 which concerned the constitutionality of the State's payment of the salaries of chaplains in secondary schools, in the light of Article 44.2.2. This provision states: 'The State guarantees not to endow any religion.' The case failed, basically, on the ground that there is less to Article 44.2.2 than meets the eye. To elaborate: the plaintiff's action failed because the Supreme Court interpreted the Constitution in the light of Irish history, which had the effect of reducing the impact of the non-endowment provision. In particular, the State's provision of education must be read in the context of a historical background in which 'the vast majority of secondary schools in this country were under the control and management of religious denominations' (at 87).

Given Ireland's troubled history of religious conflict and the contemporary turbulence in Northern Ireland, it was sensible for the judges to take the quietest line followed in these two cases, not least because this line is, one would expect, in line with the tradition of the people.

It would be easy to condemn these decisions and indeed the general notion of 'tradition and consensus' as a basis for interpreting the Constitution since, even assuming that it is possible to ascertain what tradition demands or what the national consensus is, it is evident that this approach contains an in-built bias against minorities and against change. Nevertheless, bearing in mind that judges are unelected personages, who ought to serve the needs and values of society, there is much to be said for a judicious use of this aid to interpretation.

The second tool of interpretation[4] that has emerged in the major field of fundamental rights is the principle of proportionality. To explain: none of the fundamental rights is absolute. Each contains a statement of principle restricted by exceptions, formulated in various forms of words in the Constitution, but each saying basically that the right can be qualified in the public interest. And in many cases the issue comes down to whether the law or governmental action under review goes beyond the proper balance between the principle and the exception, this balance being set by the Court interpreting the Constitution. The great question is: at what point is this balance to be drawn? This can be a rather subjective question and the significance of the doctrine of proportionality is that it provides some principled guidance in answering this query.

The classic statement of the proportionality principle is to be found in *Heaney v Ireland* [1994] 3 IR 593. This High Court case centred upon a provision of the Offences Against the State Act 1939 which made it a criminal offence for a person arrested under the Act to fail 'to give an account of their movements'. Costello J. accepted that this offence infringed the right against self-incrimination and that this right was protected by Article 38.1 ('due course of law' at criminal trial). He then continued (at 610):

> The test of proportionality contains the notions of minimal restraint on the exercise of protected rights and the exigencies of common good in a democratic

society. The objective of the impugned provision must be of sufficient importance to warrant overriding a constitutionally protected right. It must relate to concerns pressing and substantial in a free and democratic society. The means chosen must pass a proportionality test. They must:

(a)   be rationally connected to the objective and not be arbitrary, unfair or based on irrational considerations;

(b)   impair the right as little as possible, and

(c)   be such that their effects on rights are proportional to the objective.

In applying this test, Costello J. stated:

Recalling that the object which the [section] has been enacted to achieve, namely, the investigation and punishment of serious subversive crime, and having regard to the legal protections which exist which will minimise the risk involved in the operation of the section . . . it seems to me that the restriction on the right to silence imposed by the section cannot be regarded as excessive and that it is proportionate to the objective which it is designed to achieve.

Not, of course, that proportionality solves all problems. As can be seen from the passages quoted, wrapped up in the apparently objective carapace of 'proportionality' are such subjective formulae as 'proportional'; 'as little as possible'; and 'excessive'. Nevertheless, the doctrine of proportionality – which has been followed in a number of difficult cases in the 1990s – shows the judiciary respecting a sensible conceptual framework and so reducing the element of judicial subjectivity.

Concluding Comment

What this brief survey shows is that the ancient watchwords of literal interpretation established by common law judges over the centuries will no longer serve – at any rate, in an unmodified form – in the new world of constitutional review. The judges have been slow to appreciate this and thus slow to embark on the difficult work of devising more suitable alternatives. However, in the past decade, a start has been made on this task.

10. Summing Up

I. International Comparisons

The upsurge in judicial activism is certainly not peculiar to Ireland. It appears to be also very much part of the *Zeitgeist* in other countries and an illuminating comparative work, which summarizes the position in eleven states, reaches the following conclusion:

> Certain historical, structural and intellectual character-
> istics pre-conditions tend to promote the emergence of
> an activist judiciary. These characteristics are: certain
> structured and intellectual conditions which seem to
> make more likely the emergence of an activist judicia-
> ry. Among the structural features are federalism, a
> written constitution, judicial independence, a lack of
> separate administrative courts, a competitive political
> party system, and generous rules of access to the
> courts. Certain traditions, doctrines, and ideas also can
> galvanise the courts: the common law tradition, the
> concept of limited government, high esteem for judges,
> and a social consensus on fundamental constitutional
> issues . . . As the authority of legislatures, presidents,
> prime ministers, civil servants and political parties con-
> tinues to decline, there will be more and more pressure
> for the political branches of government to rely on the
> courts to make policy choices . . . Public trust in the
> judiciary is also a product of consensus on . . . the fun-
> damental constitutional issues. Where questions such
> as theocracy versus liberalism, or socialism versus cap-
> italism, remain unanswered and there is a political
> struggle among advocates of competing ways of life,
> there will be strong opponents of any policy to transfer
> responsibility for such choices to the judiciary.[1]

Despite the fact that Ireland was not one of the jurisdictions included in the study, it is striking that (apart from federalism) this paradigm fits Ireland like a glove. While for the reader who has followed me this far the parallels do not need to be laboured, one ought to emphasize the last two points: politicians and the political system are (whether deservedly or not) very unpopular in Ireland and particularly so at the present time. And, as to the final point in the question – on consensus regarding fundamental issues – one can say that there is still a fair measure of this in Ireland and also that the judges have been fairly careful to arrange their judgments so as to accord with the outlook of society. For it is appropriate in a democracy that judges should reflect the needs and values of the society whence they come and which, ultimately, they serve (a point glancingly considered at pp. 100–1).

II Stock-Taking

The burden of the message which emerges from earlier chapters is that Irish judges have, over the past thirty or so years, been notably activist. One can emphasize this point, too, by drawing comparisons. The radicalism of this switch to judicial activism in constitutional jurisprudence is remarkable, especially when set against the conservatism of the public service during almost the entire period from Independence to the present. It is a truism that until the reforms of the 80s and 90s the Irish civil service was merely a scaled down version of the civil service which Britain devised to rule a world empire. Thus, for instance, the Ombudsman was a well known institution, established in Scandinavia in the nineteenth century, yet it was only introduced here in 1980. By contrast, the judiciary had laid the foundation stones of an active form of judicial review at least as early as the 1960s (*Ryan v A.G.* [1965] IR 294). Moreover, this was at a time when there were remarkably few charts to offer guidance to Irish judges in this novel intellectual voyage. By contrast, for instance, when the Canadian judiciary were confronted by the Charter of

Rights, they already had their failed experiment with a Bill of Rights as well as the long experience of their neighbour to the south to guide them. In implementing the Human Rights Act 1998, British judges have the fairly intimate and lengthy involvement with both European Courts (European Court of Justice and European Court of Human Rights) to draw upon. All that Irish judges had (apart from, in most cases, a rather patchy knowledge of the jurisprudence of the U.S. Supreme Court) was their own ideas or those of counsel.

One of the ways in which the engine of judicial activism has been strengthened is by a significant diminution in such traditional formulae of judicial self-abnegation as *locus standi* (pp. 75–6) and the rules of judicial modesty associated with the Separation of Powers (p. 92). In addition, the presumption of constitutionality has been given a new twist to widen the reach of the judges' authority.[2] Finally, of vastly greater significance than is often noticed by legal writers is the question of the award of legal costs. Where it is the State which is a successful defendant the State is seldom awarded its own costs (in contrast to the usual practice) and is sometimes even required to pay those of the unsuccessful plaintiff. A recent example concerns the taxi drivers' action to oppose regulations freeing the market in taxi licences. Despite the fact that the taxi drivers had already lost in a related hearing and appeared to have a rather weak case, it is reported that the State was ordered to pay half their legal costs.[3] Such a practice naturally encourages litigation in the constitutional field.

The previous chapters, which may be regarded on one level as being in the nature of an audit, show how much has been done by the judges to shape the modern Irish polity and how much of it is to the good. In the first place, a thorough job has been done in removing anomalies from the law, many of them centuries old and without any reasonable justification. Examples from the public law field include Crown privileges such as that barring action against the state in tort; the privilege against the disclosure of official evidence; and the presumption that the

State was not bound by statute. And in the field of private law there have been improvements in limitations law and restrictions on court reporting.

Secondly, the judges have taken a strong line in keeping the State and its agencies under the law. This has been true in such traditional areas as personal liberty and criminal law. In addition, reforms have been made in the critical area of elections and referenda. And the biggest area of all, so far as most people's everyday lives are concerned, is 'the administrative state'. Here, too, there has been great progress in ensuring a regular process and procedure. Given the conventional decency of most public servants and the politicians who, at some point, control them, the likely outcome of this is the achieving of administrative justice. It has to be said though, that, especially because of the rather courtcentric view of the Separation of Powers which has been taken, an unnecessary inflexibility has been built in at some points.

The judges' strong instinct for fairness has led to a number of decisions protecting groups likely to be disadvantaged, among them women, itinerants and (perhaps most likely of all) suspected criminals. In the field of religion, certain low-level instances of discrimination have been quashed.

All this is to the good. However, there have been a number of major areas – admittedly particularly difficult areas – in which judicial activism has taken the form of the judiciary imposing basic policy values in preference to those chosen by the elected organs of government. More specifically, as we have seen, there have been several marginal decisions in which the values of the individual – mainly property, the right to earn a livelihood, privacy or reputation – have been preferred to the interests of the community and the State. There appear to be two positive and two negative reasons for this stance.

First, as drafted, the Constitution is a strongly individual document and, consequently, if it is given a stringent application, it will have a pro-individual effect. As Dr Hogan remarks from a slightly broader perspective, 'The nature of judicial review is that the courts are required to focus on the operation of the law as it affects the individual plaintiff and do not, generally speaking, have the capacity to examine how such a law impacts on the public at large'.[4] Thus, in the aggregate, a wave of judicial activism will inevitably have the effect of being pro-individual. However, it is also true that there are some provisions of the Constitution which could have been built upon to strengthen the position of the community. Thus we have noticed, in Chapter 4, parts I and VI, that the rights to equality and (to a lesser degree) to free speech have not been allowed the influence which they might have been given. Again, in both the defamation and the public inquiry cases, emphasis could have been placed by the judges on such (admittedly general) provisions of the Constitution as Article 1 (Ireland is 'a democratic republic') and Article 6 (the sovereignty of the people). These provisions could have been drawn upon to establish a broad doctrine of the openness, integrity and accountability of institutions and their chiefs. But no such general doctrine has developed, mainly because of the judges' concentration on individual rights.

The fact that the Constitution does not give the community any positive rights will also be significant in the context of the anticipated establishment of the European Convention of Human Rights as part of domestic law. For if the ECHR gives an individual a right (it may be to the prejudice of the community) which the Constitution does not establish, then the ECHR will not operate and the individual will succeed. If, by contrast, the individual right is in the Constitution, then even if the Convention includes an exception or limitation favouring the community the Constitution and, consequently, the individual will prevail. Heads the individual wins; tails the community loses.

Secondly, there is what one might expect to be the outlook of the typical judge. When fine choices have to be made and there is no precedent to serve as a guide, it is inevitable that a judge's value system will exert some influence. One of the most brilliant jurists to sit on the U.S. Supreme Court, Benjamin Cardozo, put the matter in these words:

> There is in each of us a stream of tendency, whether you choose to call it philosophy or not, which gives coherence and direction to thought and action. Judges cannot escape that current any more than other mortals. All their lives, forces which they do not recognise and cannot name, have been tugging at them – inherited instincts, traditional beliefs, acquired convictions; and the result is an outlook on life, a conception of social needs, a sense in James' phrase of 'the total push and pressure of the cosmos', which, when reasons are nicely balanced, must determine where choice shall fall.

The relevance of this passage in the present context is that the judges are drawn from the professional middle classes. A related point is that all senior judges have been drawn from the Bar, a small, intimate society with a long conservative tradition as a 'free profession' which goes back to the thirteenth century, long before the era of modern government. In addition, there is the stark sense of individual responsibility, which is endemic in the work of an advocate. Inevitably, these three factors mean that the typical judge's 'stream of tendency' is in favour of the individual rather than the community or the State.

Take, finally, the two negative factors mentioned earlier. The difficulties under discussion here are not novel and, classically, two bulwarks against them, or at least ways of minimizing them, have been developed, namely the doctrine of precedent and following of uniform rules of interpretation (Chapters 2 and 9, respectively). This point scarcely requires emphasis: the expression 'a government of laws, not of men' is most commonly used in relation to the executive organ and the need to subject it to the Rule of Law. But, in fact, it is just as important (if for slightly different reasons) that the judges should be governed by the law, rather than by what, based on their individual viewpoints, they consider moral or appropriate. The reason is that the judges' legitimacy, i.e. their claim on public respect for their position and obedience to their judgments depends upon the fact that they administer, consistently and impartially, an accessible body of generally accepted rules and justify their decisions by reference to these rules, in a reasoned judgment. This is vital for a peaceful society because it is the reason why court decisions are accepted with resignation by the losing party, whether a private individual or some organ of the State.

However, in what may be regarded as striking failures of judicial craftsmanship, these bulwarks have been eroded. The discipline of following precedent has not always been honoured. Likewise, there has been a failure to state and follow uniform rules for the interpretation of the Constitution, though certain cases in the 1990s demonstrate an appreciation of the issue at stake and a willingness to think out appropriate rules of interpretation.

Let us attempt to summarize the pros and cons of the sort of constitutional cases discussed in this book. In the first place, the gain from an engaged independent judiciary is beyond dispute. It can be illustrated, for instance, by the cases outlined earlier showing how the judiciary has modernized the law where the legislature has failed to do so, or has protected some (possibly unpopular) minority group to whose needs the mainstream political establishment pays insufficient attention. However, as against this, judicial activism (as defined at pp. 7–8) involves the making of policy choices by the judge involved in a case. Such a making of policy choices should be avoided, as far as possible – and that last phrase represents a considerable qualification – since it is a bad thing for the institution of the judiciary. It is bad simply because the greatest asset which the judiciary possesses is the public's faith that it decides cases on the basis of fixed and clearly-declared principles which have been set on a non-partisan basis. If the judiciary is obliged (or chooses) to haul out into broader political waters to decide a case, where inherently there can be no fixed principles, then this vital capital asset of the judiciary (and, more widely, of the institutions of an ordered, just society) is diminished. Kelly, Hogan and Whyte (Preface, *xciii*) make a rather similar point:

> Not least because all of these judgments were of major constitutional, political and social importance, it behoves the judiciary to draw on a consistent seam of constitutional doctrine. If such important and far-reaching decisions as these cannot be rationalised in conventional legal terms – by reference to objective legal principles such as precedent and other accepted sources of law – this may well lead to the politicisation of constitutional law and adjudication.

The reader who has followed me this far may well object that the cloven hoof is showing through and that what all this really shows is a political preference on the part of the present commentator. But such an objection ignores the argument being made here, which is not that one set of political views is better than another, but rather the different argument that judicial activism is likely, at some point, to require a judge to make a political choice against the elected representatives of the people and that this is, for generally accepted reasons, a course of action only to be taken for good reason. It would plainly be undesirable if a judge were to be categorized and his or her judgments respected (or not) on the basis that s/he was (to take the example of the extradition of political prisoners) sound on the national question, or (to refer to the *Sinnott* case (at pp. 68-9)) for or against autistic people.

There is another point: inappropriate reliance on the judiciary is a bad thing also for the political system. It is a sign of an immature or decaying political system if it has to call into play the judiciary to clean out its own Augian stables. Long-term, it is bad for democracy if the citizenry, instead of relying on themselves, think that they can rely excessively on the judges.

The basic point made here is simply that, in the past, the judiciary has often overlooked these costs and, consequently, has not been sufficiently discriminating in wielding the heavy weapon of judicial review. However, in a real sense this book could be said to have a happy ending for, since the coming in 2000 of the Keane Supreme Court, there have been signs that this Court, at any rate, is becoming alert to the dangers, as well as to the potential, of judicial activism. Among these signs are: *Best*; *Re Article 26 and the Planning and Development Bill 2000*, *Sinnott*; and the scepticism about the involvement of judges in extra-curial activities (see pp. 40, 46–8, 59, 68 and 90 respectively). The Supreme Court has recently reversed the High Court in a number of significant areas (*Breathnach*, *Best*, *Brady*, and *Sinnott*, at pp. 67–8). Its outlook may therefore be expected to spread to the High Court.

III Selection of Judges

A British commentator in this field remarks apropos judicial activism: 'This notion of Platonic Guardians might seem to offer a brilliant short cut to individual, if not social, progress . . . But Platonic Guardians have to be people of exceptionally high calibre'.[5] Even if one does not go all the way with the first sentiment expressed here, it seems hard to doubt the second one: judicial activism indisputably calls for judges of exceptional quality. It also involves difficult policy choices. All this throws a sharp spotlight on the process by which judges are selected. (Not that this reaction is peculiar to Ireland: this link between the expansion of the judicial role and moves to reform the selection process can currently be seen in Britain, Canada, Australia and South Africa). One of the arguments of this pamphlet is that, going by results, appropriate thought and care has not always gone into the selection of judges and, in this section, I shall suggest some ways in which this might be improved.

Before considering improvements, one ought to summarize the existing system for selecting judges. The Constitution states that judges are appointed by the President but (the sting in the tail) on the advice of the Government. It is well known that the Government has been concerned, often in the first place, with whether a candidate has the reputation of being a supporter of the Government party or parties. Whilst, because of the strong culture of an independent judiciary and legal profession, this has not led to a servile judiciary (see pp. 10–13), nevertheless it is certainly undesirable for appointments to the judiciary to appear to be part of the political spoils system.

The coming of the Judicial Appointments Advisory Board may seem to have improved matters. Such an appearance may indeed have been the reason for its establishment (by the Courts and Court Offence Act 1995) following the amazing fall of the Reynolds Fianna Fáil–Labour Coalition in late 1994. Basically, the purpose of the Board seems to be to act as a sort of short-listing committee, weeding out inadequate aspirants for judicial office. What happens is that where there is a judicial vacancy, it is for the Board to recommend at least seven candidates whom it considers suitable for appointment (on the grounds of education, qualifications, experience and character) or such lesser number as the Board considers to be suitable for appointment. The Act states that, in deciding whom to advise the President to appoint as a judge, 'the Government shall firstly consider for appointment those persons' recommended by the Board.

The Board passed its first test in 1998: its independence was demonstrated when the Government was on the point of appointing a candidate whom the Board did not consider suitable. The Board confidentially threatened to resign if the appointment went ahead and the Government climbed down. Nevertheless, these reforms seem to be rather limp and inadequate. In the first place as just indicated, the Board is far from having the power to select a judge. It merely nominates a list of seven – yes, seven! – candidates from which the Government may – but is not legally obligated to – select the appointee. Secondly, the scheme does not extend at all to the selection of the Chief Justice or the Presidents of the other courts. Nor does the scheme apply where it is a judge (from a lower court) who is the appointee. Thirdly, the composition of the Board leaves, in my opinion, a lot to be desired.[6] It is top-heavy with judges and has too few lay persons. Next, such a matter as the procedure for appointing judges is important enough to be the subject of a Constitution and not a mere statute. Finally, to mention the central subject here, the problem of ascertaining the attitude of a candidate for the High or Supreme Court to the judge's role in striking down laws is simply not addressed.

How can the machinery for this most important selection process be improved? This issue may be approached on four levels. In the first place, something must be done about the appointing agency. Both because of the excessive involvement of party politics and because government ministers have not time or expertise to do the job properly, the present role retained by the Government, even post 1995, is too great. I put it thus cautiously because it may be well be inappropriate in a democracy to remove the selection of judges altogether from the elected representatives of the people. But – to go back to my central criticism – a choice from among seven nominees leaves the Government with much too wide a discretion; given the ballyhoo with which it was established in the aftermath of the appointment of the Attorney General as President of the High Court, it is (as Aesop remarked in another context) scarcely credible that the mountain should have produced such a mouse. At the very least, the number of qualified candidates recommended by the Advisory Board from among whom the Government must ordinarily select should be reduced to two or three. These are numbers with which the Government can live in analogous systems of appointment, which also involve a politically neutral short-listing committee, with the ultimate selection being taken by the Government. Examples include the systems for selecting the Director of Public Prosecutions, higher civil servants of government departments or members of Bord Pleanála.

Secondly, take the size of the pool from which judges are selected. Since experienced practitioners are relatively few, the pool of suitable candidates is often dangerously small, especially when one takes into account the fact (mentioned elsewhere) that appointees are usually supporters of the Government

party(ies); and the fact that many eminently suitable practitioners rule themselves out because of the drop in remuneration
which judicial appointment brings. But undoubtedly the
strongest factor here is the way in which (save for District
Judges) solicitors were ruled out as candidates. The importance
of this lies in the fact that there are currently only 1,000 or so
practising barristers (of whom it happens that a disproportion-
ately large number are too young for appointment), but 6,500
solicitors. The 1995 Act[7] only lifted the ban to the extent of
allowing solicitors to be appointed directly to the Circuit Court,
but only thereafter, as a promotion, to the higher courts. We are
promised that the law will be changed to allow the appointment
of solicitors directly to the higher courts. But it will naturally take
some years for this long overdue improvement to work through
the system and there are presently (mid 2001) no former solicitors out of twenty-six Circuit Court judges and none in the higher
courts. (One should add another less important factor. This is the
total overlooking of academic lawyers which has meant one
huge loss, namely that the Bench was deprived of the services
of John Kelly, a pillar of learning and common sense, who would
have been a great asset during the 1970s and 80s, at a time of
rapid, probably too rapid, Constitutional law-making.)

Thirdly, better information on each candidate is readily available and ought to be obtained. These sources would include, in
addition to the Attorney General who is already involved, the
Director of Public Prosecutions, the Chief State Solicitor, and the
State Solicitors in each county. Ireland is a small country and
the legal professions are well structured, with various representative bodies made up of usually conscientious and perceptive
people, who are in frequent contact with the candidates for
office. I am thinking here of such bodies as the Law Society and
its provincial associations, like the Southern Law Association,
the Bar Council, the growing range of specialized groups like
the tax lawyers or family lawyers and the Irish Association of
Law Teachers. An argument might also be made for including
groups of lay persons, though a conservative counter-argument

(which appeals to this writer) could be made based on the fact that such groups would lack the necessary intimate knowledge of the candidates.

Action on any of these fronts would be relatively straight-forward and would effect a great improvement. The fourth point is more difficult. In the selection of a judge at any level, it is plain that s/he should possess qualities of integrity, wisdom, indepen-dence, fairness, good judgement, humanity, courtesy, open-mindedness and knowledge of, and commitment to admin-istering the law. Whilst the presence of such qualities to a sufficient quantity is not common, its existence (or not) is – at least within limits – a reasonably objective matter and, therefore, ought not to cause controversy. But in the case of the superior courts (High and Supreme Courts), which are both the principal law-making courts and the only courts with the power to wield the Constitution to strike down laws or governmental action, additional qualities are required. Since these tasks involve in substance law-making or law-breaking, it would seem that the democratic ideal requires that at the stage of selecting a judge it should be asked by some responsible body whether s/he possesses an understanding of, and sympathy for, the needs and values of the wider society on which his judgments will impact.

There are immense problems with such an examination of a candidate's views. One practical difficulty in Ireland would be getting the information on which to cross-examine since, on the whole, practising lawyers here do not publish their views in the same way as do candidates for (say) the U.S. Supreme Court. But the critical problem is how such an examination could be recon-ciled with the independence of the judiciary, for if the judicial candidate does not evade the question, he may be driven to adopt a position in regard to (say) abortion, private property, free speech or taxation. Then, if and when such an issue comes up for resolution before him as a judge, he certainly will not be seen to be independent. He will be perceived – and this is the absolute worst thing to say of a judge – as not being open to arguments which contradict the position on which he was elected, perhaps even as being a spokesperson for a particular segment of public opinion.

This particular issue was considered by the Constitutional Review Group (Pn 2632, 1996) which addressed the possibility of adopting the U.S. model. In the U.S. system, appointments to the Supreme Court are made by the President but must also be confirmed by the Senate, following public questioning of the candidate before the Senate Judicial Committee. The Constitutional Review Group rejected this model on the following grounds (at 180–81):

> The contemporary U.S. experience of public hearings . . . [shows that] such a process could create a situation where opposition groups or the media could attempt to discredit a candidate selected by the Government as a means of discrediting the Government. In addition, attempts have often been made to ascertain the value systems of candidates prior to appointment. This tendency is not helpful because it proceeds from an assumption that the candidate for judicial office ought to reflect in office some predetermined views considered suitable by those making the appointment. Finally, the intense public scrutiny of candidates is likely to deter the sort of people who would be suitable appointees.

These seem to me to amount to sensible reasons for rejecting the U.S. system, with its public questioning by a committee of politicians.

However, this still leaves the original problem, which the CRG, having dipped its toe in the water, pursued no further. What is suggested here is that there should be a more representative committee than the presently constituted Judicial Appointments Advisory Board, which would question a judicial candidate, in private, as to his views on the sort of approach to be taken to the striking down of laws or governmental actions. The difficulty would be to ensure that the questions did not go so far as to require a judge to commit himself as to the stance he would adopt when a concrete case came before him. The same difficulty naturally arises elsewhere and, in the context of the South African Judicial Service Commission, it has been explained:

> Guidelines drawn up by the Commission in response to concerns that candidates would be exposed to improper questioning stress the importance of restraint. They state that the function of the interviews is primarily to identify positive characteristics rather than negative ones. No questions can be asked which would require a commitment as to how a judge would decide a particular issue should it come before the court. Questions must be relevant to the selection criteria, and any questions which affect the 'reputation or dignity or . . . privacy' of the candidate should be referred to the Chairperson.[8]

Guidelines of this broad type might seem to be necessary here in Ireland if reforms of the character just recommended were produced. Admittedly, they involve fine distinctions. But, after all, lawyers are practised in making and operating fine distinctions.

Notes and References

INTRODUCTION

1   Bowles, *Government and Politics of the United States*, 2nd edn (London: Macmillan, 1998) p. 181.

2   The new members are: Murray J. (10 September 1999); McGuiness J. (9 February 2000); Hardiman J. (9 February 2000); Geoghegan J. (9 February 2000); Fennelly J. (13 March 2000). Keane C. J. was appointed 30 January 2000.

1. JUDICIAL ACTIVISM

1   See Kelly, Hogan and Whyte, *The Irish Constitution,* 3rd edn, (Dublin: Butterworths, 1994), pp. 563–64. Hereafter Kelly, Hogan and Whyte.

2   J. Grey, *Times Literary Supplement*, 15 January 2001 (book review of J. Grey, *Equality*).

3   Though, see, Murphy J. in *D.P.P. v Best* [2000] 2 ILRM 1, 35.

4   This paragraph draws on: Quinn, 'The Nature and Significance of Critical Legal Studies' (1989) 7 ILT 282; Whyte, 'Ideology and Access to the Courts', in Whelan (ed.) *Law and Liberty in Ireland* (OakTree Press, 1993).

5   It is remarkable how relatively late even judges themselves were to recognize this topic as worthy of thought. For instance, in early 1978, the present writer attended two meetings of UCC Law Student Society, each of which was addressed by a leading judge. In each, roughly the same question was put, relating to the possible dangers of judicial activism. Costello J. responded reasonably enough: 'We do it *faute de mieux* because the legislature itself has failed to reform an out-of-date or inappropriate law'. But Walsh J. had difficulty appreciating the question and, after some time said: 'You mean: "what is our warrant for acting in this way?" Well, I suppose, if the legislature doesn't like it, they can always pass a bill to amend the Constitution and get that enacted by way of a referendum'. And, in a similarly nonchalant view, Kenny J. remarked: 'Judges have become legislators and have the advantage that they do not have to face an opposition'. (1979) 30 NILQ 195, 196. But this was relatively early in the history of judicial activism. We shall consider in the remainder of this book, what developments there have been in understanding of judicial activism.

6   G.W. Hogan, [1999] *Bar Review*, pp. 205, 209.

119

7   'An Assessment of the Independence of the Irish Supreme Court in the Context of Constitutional Law with particular reference to the system of judicial appointments' (University of Cambridge Ph.D., 1993) 411–12.

8   Interview with Fergus Pyle, *The Irish Times,* 4 March 1987.

9   The case is *Re Art. 26 and the Housing (Private Rented Dwellings) Bill* [1983] I.R. 181, 186–7. The comment is from J. Casey, *Constitutional Law of Ireland*, 3rd edn (Dublin: Round Hall, Sweet and Maxwell, 2000), p. 334. Hereafter Casey.

10 As it happened, this opportunity (in December 1936) coincided almost exactly with Mr de Valera's abolition of the Senate and occurred only a few months before President Roosevelt's failed scheme to pack the U.S. Supreme Court.

11 Both extracts from an interview with Walsh J. in Sturgess and Chubb, *Judging the World: Law and Politics in the World's Leading Courts* (Sydney, 1988) at 418–19, quoted in Ruane, 113–14.

12 See *The Times,* 19 April 1994.

13 See (1981) ICLQ 335. (D. Gwynn Morgan).

14 G. Hogan and C. Walker, *Political Violence and the Law in Ireland* (Manchester University Press, 1989), Chapter 10.

15 See G. Hogan and D. Gwynn Morgan, *Irish Administrative Law* (Round Hall, Sweet and Maxwell), pp. 935–51.

16 *The Irish Times, 27* January 2001.

17 Some of the ideas in this section are taken from a paper given by P. Ward to the Brehon Law School, Co. Clare on 1 May 1998. See, too, G.W. Hogan, 'Irish Nationalism as a Legal Ideology' (1986) Studies 10.

2. THE COMMON LAW JUDGE

1   'The Judge as Law-Maker' XII (1972) JSPTL 22, 22.

2   For an account of the stages of evolution, see B. McMahon and W. Binchy, *The Law of Torts*, 3rd edn, (Dublin: Butterworths, 2000), Chapter 12.

3   *Devanney v Minister for Justice* [1998] ILRM 81 and *Tang v Minister for Justice* [1996] 2ILRM46 (at 6–7); *Byrne v Ireland* [1972] IR241 and *Webb v Ireland* [1988] IR353, analysed in D. Gwynn Morgan, 'Constitutional Interpretation' (1988) 10 DULJ 24. For the extraordinary gyrations in the interpretation of 'political offence' in the Extradition Act 1965, see e.g. G. Hogan and C. Walker, *Political Violence and the Law in Ireland*, pp. 288–90.

4   'Implications for the Practising Lawyer' in D. Moloney and M. Robinson (eds), *The Brussels Convention on Jurisdiction and the Enforcement of Foreign Judgments* (I.E.E.L., 1989). See, to like effect J. Mee, 'Taking precedent seriously' (1993) I.L.T. 254.

5   F. McAuley and P. McCutcheon, *Criminal Liability* (Round Hall, Sweet and Maxwell, 2000), p. x.

3. SEXUAL AND SOCIAL MORES

1   S. McDonagh (ed.), *The Attorney General v X and Others* (Incorporated Council of Law Reporting for Ireland, 1992).

2   From Kelly, Hogan and Whyte's exemplary treatment of this subject.

3   The President of Ireland, Mrs Robinson, remarked publicly: '. . . I hope we have the courage which we have not always had . . ., to say this is a problem we have got to resolve'. [O. O'Leary and H. Burke, *Mary Robinson* (Dublin: Sceptre Lir, 1998), p. 102.

4   On which, see J. Casey, *Constitutional Law of Ireland* 3rd edn (Dublin: Round Hall, Sweet and Maxwell), pp. 201–03

5   A. O'Halloran, *Adoption: Law and Practice* (Dublin: Butterworth 1992), Foreword, vii.

6   See A. Shatter, *Family Law in the Republic of Ireland* 4th edn, (Dublin: Butterworths) pp. 500–02. In *WOR v EH* [1996] 2IR 248 a majority of the Supreme Court refused to follow *Keegan,* holding that Article 41 does not protect de facto family ties.

7   See *Doyle v Minister for Education* Supreme Court, 21 December 1995; *Re O'Brien* [1954] IR 1; *K.C. and A.C. v An Bord Uchtála* [1985] ILRM 302, 317.

8   Shatter, p. 491.

4. SOCIAL REFORMING LEGISLATION

1   Casey, p. 450.

2   Subsequently, reformulated versions of these measures, designed to take account of flaws discovered in the original legislation, were enacted. Their constitutionality has not been tested.

3   I. Lynch, 'The Right to Freedom of Association in the Irish Constitution' in T. Murphy and P. Twomey (eds), *Ireland's Evolving Constitution* (Oxford: Hart Publishing, 1998).

4   Lynch, p. 226.

5   See Kelly, Hogan and Whyte op. cit., 1055–6; Osborough, (1978) 13

Ir. Jur. 145, 173. A similar comment could be made about the adoption authorities analysed at pp. 30–4 above.

6   For a general account, see Hogan, Whyte and Kelly pp. 1061–91.

7   See, to like effect, *In re Viscount Securities* (1978) 112 ILTR 17.

8   *Report of Committee on the Price of Building Land*. (Prl. 3632).

9   The Report's recommendations also involve a Separation of Powers point: because of the exact, legal terms (necessitated by respect for the property right) in which the main recommendation was cast, it was feared that the decision (as to whether the land's value had been increased by local authority works) would amount to an 'administration of justice'. If so, then the Separation of Powers (Article 34.1) would require that the decision should be vested in a court and not in some administrative body (such as a local authority). In other words, the critical point here is one of legal classification, namely that the Committee anticipated (in line with a steady stream of judicial authority) that, despite the fact that compulsory acquisition was a matter of public administration, it was to be regarded also as an administration of justice. Hence, a court had to be involved and, presumably, it had to be the High Court because compulsory acquisition is rather draconian – though this is a political, rather than a legal point. The net result is that the scheme would have been a rather cumbersome one which would have made a local authority very slow to use it.

10 'The Irish Constitution in its Historical Context', in T. Murphy and P. Twomey (eds), *Ireland's Evolving Constitution 1937–1997* (Oxford: Hunt, 1998). See also Constitutional Review Group (Pn. 2632, 1996) pp. 366–67. See, too, *Dáil Debates* vol. 345, col. 666 (25 Oct. 1983). McCormack, 'Blake-Madigan and its Aftermath' (1983) 5 DULJ 205, 223, 'There has been a beatification of the market economy through the Constitution'.

11 *Land Use, Compensation and the Community* (1983) 18 Ir. Jur.23, 32–33.

12 Again, in *Air Canada v U.K.* [1995] 20 EHRR 150, a somewhat similar case, the European Court of Human rights found for the Government of the U.K. by five to four, with the Irish judge, Walsh J., voting with the dissentients.

13 Casey, 2nd edn, p. 547.

14 Contrast and option issued at p. 33.

15 [1999] 4 IR 432. *Hynes-O'Sullivan v. O'Driscoll* [1988] IR 436 is another example in which an opportunity to use the Constitution to rein in the libel law was rejected. According to the leading commentator on defamation, the Court did not 'attempt to determine the "due balancing" of the various rights needed to ensure the constitutionality of the general structure of the qualified privilege defence' (M. McDonald, 11 [1989] DULJ 94, 106). Notice too that in an early case a journalist's right to protect his sources was rejected (*In Re O'Kelly* [1974] 108 ILTR 97). For proposals for reform, see Law Reform Commission. *Report of the Civil Law of Defamation* (1991). *De Rossa* was, in substance, confirmed by the Supreme Court itself in *O'Brien v The Irish Mirror* 25 October 2000.

16 cp. 'The limits of acceptable criticism are . . . wider as regards a politician as such than as regards a private individual. Unlike the latter, the former inevitably and knowingly lays himself open to close scrutiny of his every word and deed by both journalist and the public at large, and he must consequently display a greater degree of tolerance' (*Lingens v Austria* [1986] 8 EHRR 407 at para. 42).

17 G. Quinn, 'Judicial Activism under the Irish Constitution' (paper given to University of San Sebastian Summer School, 6 July 2000) p.40. The next two paragraphs draw fairly heavily on Dr Quinn's analysis.

18 See Kelly, Hogan and Whyte pp. 400–07 outlining several cases in which claims based on laws providing for hearings *in camera* have been rejected.

5. PUBLIC INQUIRIES: THE PEOPLE'S RIGHT TO KNOW

1 For further details, see Hogan and Morgan, pp. 293–311.

2 The three non-judicial inquiries referred to are: the non-statutory Hepatitis C Expert Group (1995); the Dáil Inquiry into the fall of the Fianna Fáil–Labour Coalition (1995); and the Dunnes Stores Tribunal (1996).

3 See e.g. *Re Haughey* [1971] IR 217, 257–60, and other cases critiqued in D. Gwynn Morgan, *The Separation of Powers in the Irish Constitution* (Dublin: Round Hall, Sweet and Maxwell, 1996), pp. 222–24.

6. TAXATION AND LARGE-SCALE PUBLIC EXPENDITURE

1 Among the other difficulties to be negotiated in this area are the issues of the comparator, i.e. with what unmarried unit is a married

couple to be compared. In *Murphy,* the court seems to have assumed that the answer was an unmarried couple who were living together, despite the fact that in the late 1970s the number of unmarried couples living together for a substantial period of time was small. It might be said, on the other hand, that if one takes two single people living separately as the basis of comparison, then their expenses are much greater and hence, the imbalance in the tax system does no more than compensate for this – but when one takes account of children (and the family provision seems to assume the existence of children) it becomes once more the case that the married state is an expensive state. But what if one is comparing a married couple which has children with a one-parent family? Without going into details (on which see Kelly, Hogan and Whyte, pp. 992–94) one can say that in *Mhic Mhathuna v Ireland* [1989]-I.R. 504, the High Court appeared to find a way of allowing the State to provide support for one-parent families that is not available to married families, without falling foul of *Murphy.*

2   *D.B. v. Minister for Justice* [1999] I IR 29 (Kelly J.); *TD v. Minister for Education Unreported High Court,* 25 February 2000 (Kelly J.); *F(N) v Minister for Education* [1995] IR 29 9 Geoghegan J.). Notice, too, *O'Donoghue v Minister for Health* [1997] 2 IR. (O'Hanlon J.), which concerned a claim that a severely mentally-disabled child was entitled to appropriate educational facilities at the State's expense, irrespective of cost. The plaintiff put his case on the basis of Article 42.4 of the Constitution by which 'The State shall provide for free primary education and shall endeavour to give reasonable aid to private and corporate educational initiative'. For comment, see B. Ruane, 2000 Bar Review 416.

3   G.W. Hogan, *The Irish Times,* 14 July 2001, p. 8. 'Unelected judges cannot remedy some wrongs only a government can put right'.

7. PROCEDURE AND PROCESS

1   Notice though that *Heaney* has in effect been reversed by the European Court of Human Rights: *The Irish Times,* 22 December 2000 ,and that a divergent note was sounded by the Supreme Court itself in *The People (DPP) v Finnerty,* S.C. 17 June 1999.

2   E.g. *McGimpsey v Ireland* [1990] IR 110; *Riordan v An Tánaiste* [1997] 3 IR 502.

3   This pregnant phrase was used in *Gallagher v The Revenue*

Commissioners (No. 1) [1991] 2 IR 370.

4   The length to which the last sentence goes is clear when one bears in mind the content of the reports which each applicant had received. One of these reports (that of the first applicant) may be quoted to illustrate their suggestively damning character: '1. *Anthony Gallagher*, I am to report that on Friday the 31st October 1986 officer A. Gallagher was on duty in the visiting box. At approx. 4.15 p. m. on the termination of inmate Kenneth Noonan's visit this inmate was allowed to leave the visiting box and escape via the main gate.' In face of this, it might be assumed by a person in the position of Prison Officer that if he had some explanation of his conduct to offer, it would be prudent to offer it. However, Blayney J. rejected such a commonsensical approach and required something more akin to a formal charge.

5   By contrast, in *R. v Boundary Commission ex p. Foot* [1983] I AER 1099, the Court of Appeal held that in English law, there was nothing to prevent differences as high as 44% from the national average.

8. THE SEPARATION OF POWERS

1   For elaboration on this chapter, see D. Gwynn Morgan, *The Separation of Powers in the Irish Constitution* (Dublin: Round Hall, Sweet and Maxwell 1996.).

2   M. Vile, *Constitutionalism and the Separation of Powers* (New York: Glencoe, 1967), p. 4.

3   See District Court clerks (at p. 3); adoption (at p. 33); and compulsory acquisition of land (at p. 120, n. 9).

4   Deloitte and Touche, *Report on Insurance in Ireland* (1996), para 5.2.5.

5   For the judiciary's membership of the Anglo-Irish Law Enforcement Commission on extradition and the conclusions which they reached, see G. Hogan and C. Walker, *Political Violence and the Law in Ireland* (Manchester University Press, 1989), pp. 285–87.

6   See Morgan, *The Separation of Powers*, pp. 222–24.

7   On this and the last point, see Kelly, Hogan and White, pp. 421–23.

8   This resulted in a glaring contradiction between *Crotty v Ireland* and *McGimpsey v An Taoiseach*. See further D. Gwynn Morgan in T. Murphy and P. Twomey (eds.), *Ireland's Evolving Constitution* (Oxford: Hart, 1998,) pp. 107–11.

9   Devlin, *The Judge* (1979: OUP) 56.

9. INTERPRETING THE CONSTITUTION

1   In D. Curtin and A. O'Keeffe (eds), *Constitutional Adjudication in European Community and National Law: Essays for the Hon. Mr. Justice T.F. O'Higgins* (1992), Chap. 14.

2   For another example of literal interpretation, involving the phrase 'inalienable and imprescriptible' in Article 41.1.1°, see pp. 31–3.

3   M. Forde, *Constitutional Law of Ireland* (Cork: Mercier 1987), pp. 73–80.

4   This and the following two paragraphs draw heavily on the seminal article by G.W. Hogan, 'The Constitution, Property Rights and Proportionality' XXXII (1997) Irish Jurist 373 in which the material in the text is worked out in more detail.

10. SUMMING UP

1   G. Stein, *Judicial Activism in Comparative Perspective* (New York: St Martin's Press, 1991), pp. 7–10. The eleven states are: U.S.A., England, Canada, Australia, Israel, Italy, France, Germany, Sweden, Japan and the Soviet Union.

2   Kelly, 458–62.

3   *The Irish Times, 24* March 2001, p 3.

4   'Property Rights and Proportionality' (XXXII) 1997 *Irish Jurist* 373, 396.

5   J.A.G. Griffith, 'The Brave New World of Sir John Laws', 2000 Modern L.R. 159, 174.

6   The Board's membership is as follows: the Chief Justice, the Presidents of the High, Circuit and District Courts, a barrister and a solicitor, nominated by their respective professional bodies; and three lay persons who have experience of commerce, finance, administration or are experienced as users of the Courts.

7   As originally published, the 1995 Act would have allowed for solicitors to be appointed to the High Court and Supreme Court. However, this was removed, before the Bill reached the Dáil, by a 'display of pyrotechnics from the Bar, which was something wonderful to behold'. (I am quoting a Department of Justice, Equality and Law Reform source here).

8   K. Malleson, 'Assessing the Performance of the Justice Service Commission' 1999 South African LJ 36, 43.